**Our Reward Will Be in History
by Willie Worsley
with Terry Mulgrew**

*To Mike
Thank you
very much
Willie Worsley
A.O.F 2007
(50th yrs was GREAT)*

Copyright © 2015 Willie Worsley and Terry Mulgrew
All Rights Reserved

This book is dedicated to all my children:

My daughter Roz (pictured left), my daughter Etta (pictured right) and my grandchildren -
Roz's children Briana, Mahogany, and Kayla
and Etta's children Michael, Nicole, and David.

I LOVE YOU ALL! WILLIE WORSLEY

Foreword

By Nate "Tiny" Archibald

Willie Worsley and I have been the best of friends since the early 1960's, and we are as close today as we have ever been. Having a friend for that long, someone you can depend upon no matter what, is a blessing. I have learned so much from Willie throughout my life, and I truly consider him one of the greatest people I have ever known.

Willie and I first connected while attending DeWitt Clinton High School in the Bronx. We were both players on the varsity basketball team, but Willie is a little older than I am and was on the team before I arrived. He was my role model. We had plenty of great players on the team, but for my money, Willie was the best. In fact, he wasn't just the best player on our team -- I think he was the best player in all of New York City. And because of that, I tried to emulate him. Willie could do it all. He could dunk. He could pass. He could score. He could guard and defend. Some players could do these things in practice, but it doesn't count in practice. It counts in the game, and Willie controlled the game. He was like a great chess player, always thinking several moves ahead of his opponent. He was our catalyst, and I always referred to him as our "quiet assassin." Willie is quiet in nature, just like me. He didn't trash talk the way a lot of players do today. He let his play do the talking. And when I was a younger player on the bench, I had the best seat in the house and learned the right way to approach basketball.

Willie and I would be teammates again after we both left Dewitt Clinton. I eventually joined him at the University of Texas, El Paso, where we played for Hall of Fame coach Don Haskins. In fact, we actually played together more in college than we did in high school. And once again, I observed him as a way of improving my play. Willie taught me how to practice. He worked at his craft. He was always conditioning, and I followed his lead. I didn't consider myself a great jumper, but Willie made me realize that if I was in great shape, I would have an advantage over my opponents. And it wasn't just the physical parts of the game I learned from Willie; it was the mental aspects as well. The most important skill in basketball doesn't come from the neck down, it comes from the neck up. People always thought Willie was undersized, and even though I'm taller than he is, some may have thought that about me too. He taught me that size does not make the player. His basketball intellect put him in the right position every time; he could match up against anyone on the planet. I saw him do it time and time again.

Basketball fans like to debate what the toughest position to play is. Is it center? Is it forward? Is it guard? To me, it can be all of these. The most difficult position is the "lead" position. If you are the lead player on the team, no matter what your position, you have the toughest job. And when I played with Willie in high school, and college, and even in the famed summer leagues at Rucker Park, he was always the lead player. And as the lead player, he taught me how to sacrifice for the team effort. This is a quality that exists in all the greats. For example, when Michael Jordan first came into the league, he was dunking the ball every chance he had, but he realized the toll this would take on his body. He changed his game for the betterment of the team, and it paid off with several championships. When Willie arrived at Texas Western he was, in my mind, the best high school scorer in all of New York City. But when Don Haskins made the team focus on defense, Willie was flexible. He didn't care about the stat sheet. He cared about winning. He has won on all courts, from the playgrounds to the pros, and winning as a team is all that has ever mattered to him.

With all his experience, I know that Willie could coach basketball on any level. But a part of me is glad that his coaching success has been at the high school level, because that is my favorite basketball. In professional basketball, money and contracts are always factors; in college basketball, scholarships and the national limelight can be factors. But high school basketball is pure. High school basketball is where you learn. High school basketball isn't about you, it's about the team. Some people think that when I made it to the pros I fulfilled my basketball dream, but that's not true, I did that when I made the team at DeWitt Clinton High School. Just making varsity was my dream. When a player does make it to the next level, a lot of that has to do with the guy on the sideline, and to me, there is no better person to learn from than Willie Worsley.

I played 14 seasons in the N.B.A. and in 1991 I was elected to the Hall of Fame. During my career as a guard, I had to manage the game. I had to find ways to get to the basket. I had to adapt to man on man coverage versus zones. I had to work on my speed and conditioning. I had to be the "lead" player at times while changing my game towards the end of my career. In my mind, my basketball partnership and lifetime friendship with Willie Worsley contributed greatly to my success.

With all the good things Willie has contributed to the world through basketball, his life has taken him in many different directions. At each stop, he has left his mark in a positive way, just the way he did every time he stepped onto the court. To me, this book is a blueprint on how to approach not only basketball, but life, the right way and to be the best you can be.

Table of Contents

Our Reward Will Be in History by Willie Worsley
with Terry Mulgrew 1
Foreword 4
Table of Contents 6
Chapter 1: The Halls 7
Chapter 2: The Beginning 9
Chapter 3: The Courts 14
Chapter 4: The Staircase 21
Chapter 5: Iron Head 31
Chapter 6: The Ties That Bind 39
Chapter 7: The Bear 47
Chapter 8: The Season 52
Chapter 9: The Ladder 62
Chapter 10: The Beauty of the Good 70
Chapter 11: Last Year and Next Year 75
Chapter 12: The Gift 80
Chapter 13: Dreams Do Come True 85
Chapter 14: The Mirror 90
Chapter 15: My Girl 102
Chapter 16: Glory Road 108
Chapter 17: The Hall 115
Chapter 18: Our Reward Will be in History 120
Chapter 19: The Greatest Game of My Life 125
Acknowledgements 127

Chapter 1: The Halls

"The hallway of every man's life is paced with pictures; ...all useful, for if we learn to be wise, we can learn from them a rich and braver way to live"
Sean O'Casey

There are amazing extremes to the typical halls of a school building. Sometimes, when students are in class or it is after school, the halls can be the quietest and most peaceful place on earth. Other times, the chaos is hard to put into words. Students are jockeying for position. Some are trying to get to class on time while others are trying to be late. Couples stroll down the halls holding hands, while others argue the hot topics of the day… who is the best rapper? Who is the best basketball team? Who is the best this and that?

I was twenty-three years old when my basketball career officially ended. The time had come for my professional life to go in a new direction. By following the desire in my heart to help people, I spent the majority of my adult life in the halls -- the halls of life.

My first stop, in 1969, was at a facility for troubled teens named Woodycrest Youth Service, located in walking distance of Yankee Stadium. From there, I went on to work at the Boys Choir of Harlem Academy. This was a performing arts not-for-profit school. I held several positions there. At one point I worked as a billing manager, but I ultimately became the Dean of Students. Here I was in charge of school safety, overseeing the halls, breaking up the occasional fight, but above all ensuring the well-being of all the students and staff.

My last stop is at Spring Valley High school, a small public school in Rockland County-- a suburb of New York City. I am proud to work here, where I serve in two capacities. I have been the head coach of the Varsity Basketball team since 2000. And in 2004, I came to the school full-time as a hall monitor. Through the years, I have met some people that have my job and do not like the term "hall monitor." They prefer security aide or security guard, but I have never considered myself a security guard. When I hear that I think of a night watchman sleeping in front of black and white security camera monitors. I don't need a title to define my role. I monitor the halls. I keep traffic moving, intervening whenever necessary, while helping students and staff in any way I can.

School halls are not the only "halls" in my life. I am a member of several halls of fame. In the 1980's, I was inducted into the Dewitt Clinton High School Hall of Fame. Clinton is where I played high school basketball. On the surface, a high school hall of fame might not seem that impressive. However, over fifteen N.B.A. players were athletes at the school. Only one school, the Oak Hill Academy in Virginia, has graduated more professionals. I am a member of the Harlem Hall of Fame. I received this honor because of humanitarian work I have done in the community and my prowess on the playground courts of Rucker Park on 155 Street and 8th Avenue. I am a member of the Brooklyn, U.S.A. Hall of Fame. This honor was also based on my playground legend, as well as the historical significance of some of the college games in which I participated. I played my college basketball in Texas, and I am a member of the Texas Black Caucus Hall of Fame. At the Downtown Athletic Club, where they award football's Heisman Trophy, I was inducted, the same year as basketball coaching legend Rick Pitino, to the New York City Hall of Fame.

There is one other Hall of Fame induction that I am particularly proud of. In 2007, I became a member of the Naismith Memorial Basketball Hall of Fame. Most people mistakenly refer to this as the N.B.A. Hall of Fame. This is basketball's highest honor. Less than 400 people have ever received a hall of fame ring from this institution, and I am one of them. Many people wonder how a member of basketball's ultimate Hall of Fame came to work as a school hall monitor. I'd love to tell you.

Chapter 2: The Beginning

"In every conceivable manner, the family is link to our past, bridge to our future."
Alex Haley

Half of what I say is meaningless
But I say it just to reach you
Julia
Julia
Julia
Ocean Child
Calls me
So I sing a song of Love
Julia

    John Lennon wrote those lyrics as a tribute to his mother Julia. If God had given me musical ability, instead of athletic ability, I would have written many songs to honor my wonderful mother. There is nothing more important to me on this planet than family. And I know in my heart that anything positive that I have ever been able to give my wife Claudia, my daughters Etta and Rosalyn, their partners in life Greg and Tony, and my grandchildren David, Nicole, Michael, Brianana, Mahogany, and Kayla, comes from the strength and love my mother instilled in me.

    Julia Worsley gave birth to me, Willie James Worsley, on December 13th, 1945 in Little Washington, North Carolina. Julia was a beautiful young lady. She had big hazel eyes, light brown skin, and a warm, reassuring smile. If you asked her, she would have said that she was five feet tall. Personally, I think it was really 4'11'' and that extra inch was something that we'd joke about all the time. My mother was a great athlete. I would hear stories about her dominating the basketball courts and loved it every time I did. Back then, on the playgrounds, basketball was much more of a half court game which was suited to someone of her petite stature. I think there is a tendency to link a son's athletic ability with his father's, but my mother and I have a lot in common physically. In my playing days, I was listed as 5'6'' 165 pounds. I don't think there is another major sport more associated with height than basketball. But just like my mother, that was not something I was going to let stop me.

    I don't remember my time in North Carolina. By the time I was three years old, we moved to Norfolk, Virginia. It was here, where I lived until I was eleven, that the foundation of who I am as a man was laid.

My father's name is Orange Buck. He had a brother named Lemon Buck. I always laugh and joke that my grandmother must have loved fruit, because those are not nicknames. Those are the names on their birth certificates.

My father Orange was also a good athlete. He played semi-pro baseball for a time. He was darker skinned than my mother and almost a full foot taller at 5'11." As I got older, many people would comment that we looked like brothers as much as father and son.

My father was out of the house for most of the time I lived in Virginia. I don't know if it was ever official, like a legal separation, but he lived on his own. In fact, at some point years down the line he started a second family and fathered my half sister Samantha and my half brother William. They were good people and later on in life, when I would visit Norfolk, I could always tell that they were proud of my accomplishments and that they bragged about me to anyone who would listen.

Being an only child raised alone by my mother is part of the reason my mother meant the world to me. She was my world. We lived in the top floor of a small house in a one bedroom apartment. We did not have a bathroom. There was an outhouse around back for us to use. We didn't even know our neighbors and there weren't any local children for me to play with. My mother was not just my parent, but my best friend. We didn't have a television and many of my nights were spent enjoying my mother teaching me how to dance. To this day, I still love to "shake the tail-feather" as she used to say. I think I passed my love of dance down to my daughter Roz.

My mother was the hardest working person I have ever met. She never missed work. She never called in sick. I believe the work ethic I have had in life as a student, player, coach, and in other areas of my professional life, all comes from her. "A decent days work for a decent days pay" were words she lived by.

It was the early 1950's, and my mother's main source of income was to work as a maid. She would walk for miles, or when she could afford it take a bus, from our all black community to the all white community across town. At night, she would go to work at a Chinese Restaurant and repeat this cycle each day of the week.

These circumstances certainly taught me to be self-sufficient and get old quickly. When I entered the first grade, there were no school buses to take me to school. Without options, I would walk two and a half miles to school every day. This was no easy task. I had to cross the Tidewater Drive, a four lane highway, to make it to John T. West Elementary School.

I got very good grades when I was in high school. However, I was not a great student in elementary school. I talked fast and I stuttered, so I would do anything I could not to get called on in class. School recess really provided me with my only interaction with anyone my age. My athletic ability started to show and I won Most Outstanding Player through a Pop Warner football league connected with the school. But even with this time to play with kids my age, I was aloof and socially withdrawn. Other kids did not outwardly pick on me because of my speech impediment. I have always been a tough person, and the other kids instinctively knew things would not end well for them if they tried to bully me. But my physical toughness didn't change my shy interior. I mostly kept to myself.

On weekends, my mother had no choice but to take me with her to her job as a maid across town. She was very protective of me. I was her only child and small for my age. If she could help it, she didn't want me to be left alone in our tiny apartment all day. With no bathroom, I couldn't even stay inside if I wanted to. When we arrived at the houses she cleaned, I was hustled into the kitchen to help out the staff while she worked. It was an unspoken rule that the people of the house were not to see me there. In the kitchen, I would spend the day peeling potatoes or helping with the cooking in some other way. I never saw my mother mistreated by her white employers, or treated kindly either. I would never go against what my mother told me, so I never left the kitchen. However, although my mother never complained, my guess would be that she was treated the way most black maids were treated before the civil rights movement of the 1960's started to slowly change things.

As I approached eleven years old, my mother decided we needed to move from Norfolk, Virginia in an attempt to better our situation. She left for the Morrisina Avenue, St. Mary Park area of the Bronx, New York to prepare our new home. I became the man of the house—the man of the house of one. She left me money for food, and I stayed behind for five days all by myself.

Eventually, my aunt put me on a bus for the Port Authority in New York City. My mother gave me very specific instructions for my trip. I was not to move a muscle as I looked out the window of the bus. Young people tend to take everything so literally that this is exactly what I did. I'm surprised they didn't need a crowbar to pry me from my seat when I finally hit New York.

When I arrived, I saw my mother and a man I didn't recognize. He seemed to recognize me. It was my father, Orange Buck. He and my mother decided to make another go of their relationship. He was the love of her life, and even his leaving us before wasn't enough to make her stop loving him.

Like most people who come to a big city for the first time, I could not believe the size of the buildings. I certainly never saw anything like them in Norfolk, Virginia. When we arrived at our new apartment, I think I would have believed it if you told me we had won the lottery. We had two bedrooms, beautiful floors, and a bathroom with a tub. In Virginia, our apartment was on the second floor. Now we were so far up in the sky that I could look down and see the subways passing by. This eventually worked out great for me. I could wait until I saw a subway car approaching and then run down the stairs of the building and catch a train to school.

My mother once again worked as a maid to help support us. My father took work at a printer shop and sometimes would take me with him for the extra income. I did this without my mother's knowledge because she would not have approved of the hours. We arrived at the shop around 3 a.m. and put the names of stores on plastic shopping bags. From there, I would go straight to school. These were not ideal hours for a student, but I wanted to help the family any way I could.

This went on for about three years until my parents split up again for good. They would fight constantly and I knew in my heart that this situation was not going to last. And this was, in essence, the end of me and my father as well. Sometimes in divorce children are forced to take sides. My mother was my life, and maybe my father knew I was hers. Besides one interaction when I was in college, we didn't see each other again.

When I was about fifty years old, and working at Spring Valley High School, someone, who has long since retired from the school, approached me with a phone message. "Willie, we just got a phone call. Your father died." I could not believe the insensitivity in which the message was delivered. It was so matter of fact and void of any emotion. At that point, for years, I had considered trying to reach out to my father. I wanted to clean the slate. I didn't want to hang out, or have dinner, or start us having daily phone calls. I just wanted to tell him that I thought, on some level, he did the best he could. I guess it would have been an act of forgiveness on my part. I wanted to tell him that I loved him. Good, bad, or indifferent, he was the only father I will ever have-- even though he was incapable of being a dad.

My father leaving my mother and me, in New York City, was a whole different ballgame compared to leaving us in the country setting of Virginia. This was much worse. It was a body blow to me and my mother.

We really struggled to make ends meet. My mother again added a job at a Chinese restaurant, and I took on a paper route, but money was tight. Eventually, we had no choice but to apply for welfare. The welfare office really opened my young eyes to some of the ways of the world. We'd wait for two hours on line just to get the form we needed. Then we'd sit down and have to fill out an hour of repetitive questions. When we'd get back on line they would tell us we needed this or that or make up some reason why the form was done incorrectly. I realized that they were going to do anything possible to come up with an excuse not to give us the assistance we desperately needed. It was the first time in my life I thought "to hell with the system" and it wouldn't be the last.

We survived. It was always my mother and I against the world and if we had each other, we could get through it all. And as I reflect on my life, and think about how important my mother was to me, and how important basketball has been to me, it is amazing that my mother only saw me play once. Through hundreds of high school games, and college games, and some games in the A.B.A, there was only one time she allowed herself to miss work and watch.

It happened on March 19th, 1966. My mother put on a small black and white television in our Bronx apartment and watched the national broadcast. I was playing for the N.C.A.A Division 1 Men's Basketball Championship.

Chapter 3: The Courts

"Now there's a new skyline in Harlem
It's rising tall and free—
And if it keeps on rising
There'll be a brand new me"
                               -Langston Hughes

If someone ever asks you what the most common religion in New York City is, realize that it is a trick question. Whatever faith popped into your head as the answer, be aware that the real answer is basketball. For people of the inner city, street-ball is more than just a game. It is a way of life. And all the people who have ever dreamed of playing in the N.B.A might not realize something that I know in my heart to be true. Breaking in and making it on the courts of New York City is just as hard as joining the professional ranks.

I've heard that moving is one of the most stressful events people face in life. If that is true, try to imagine what I was going through as a shy, thirteen year-old kid from the South now immersed in the concrete jungle of New York.

My initial attraction to basketball actually had nothing to do with a love of the game. In fact, even though I was a good athlete with some success at football while living in Virginia, I had never played basketball a single time before arriving in New York. I had two ulterior motives to give basketball a try. I was always a quiet, somewhat withdrawn child. I thought that if I was able to play basketball, the dominant sport of my new surroundings, I could make some friends. The other practical reason to succeed at basketball was my own safety. There were a lot of gangs where I lived, and that was never going to be me. Knowing I would never join a gang, I figured that if gang members knew me from the courts, they would be cool with me when I walked to and from school everyday.

When reading the story of someone with a Basketball Hall of Fame ring, you might think I walked right onto the courts and showed everyone I was a star. That did not even come close to happening. At 5'6," I couldn't even get onto the court. People would look at me, with my height, and assume I was terrible. And at that point, they were right. I couldn't get better watching from the sidelines, but that is where I always remained. The pecking order on New York City basketball courts is sacred. The winners rule with no questions asked. There is no chalkboard to sign up for next game. There is no one going around asking who has or hasn't had a chance to play yet. If you won, you got to pick your team and presided over all elements of the game— including the new opposing captain. The winning team could veto the picks of the new captain. It may seem like the winners would want to play bad players, but there was no honor in that.

Frustrated and dejected, one day I somehow made my way over to the handball courts. I'm glad I did. Eugene, four years older than me, and Donald, two years older than me, invited me to join them for a game. Eventually, Gene and Donald would introduce me to their sisters Delores and Teresa and these friendships would stay with me a lifetime for two important reasons. First, they are all really great people. Second,
they are also my in-laws. I married their sister Claudia and in the summer of 2014, we celebrated our 50th wedding anniversary.

Handball actually really helped me develop skills that translated over to the basketball court. The object of the game is to throw a small, pink ball against the concrete wall and get it past your opponent. If it bounces twice before your competition can return it you get a point. Playing handball improved my lateral movement dramatically, and moving your feet from side to side quickly is so important in basketball.

As I got better at handball, I eventually moved on to the similar sport of paddle ball. This sport uses a smaller ball and wooden rackets, but the rules are mostly the same. New York City is a melting pot, and even though I lived in a predominantly Spanish neighborhood the paddle ball courts saw people of all races and cultures having fun together without conflict. All that mattered to the players there was skill, not color. When I'd eventually play for Hall of Fame Basketball coach Don Haskins, I'd realize that he had a similar mindset.

The older paddle ball players were in their thirties and forties. As kids, we couldn't afford rackets but they would let us borrow theirs from time to time. I think it was fun for them to pass on the love of a sport that they enjoyed so much. Occasionally, they would let us keep the beat up paddles that were on their last legs. We'd find black electrical tape and try to fix them up enough to use. Through practice, I slowly got better and better.

Eventually, I got very good and was confident enough to challenge the old timers. How could I lose? There was no way they could keep up with the cardiovascular abilities of an athletic teenager. I could not have been more wrong. They had me running around the court like a rabbit. They'd make me run from side to side. They'd force me to switch hands to keep me off balance. They used their experience to take away my athletic strengths. As embarrassing as it was at the time to lose to men I considered over the hill, looking back I'm glad it happened. It taught me valuable lessons, and not just on humility. It showed me the importance of strategy in sport. They moved without moving. They used and conserved energy at the same time. They were good athletes, but their game plan was why they won. This knowledge helped me on the basketball court as a player. And later on in life, this lesson still resonates with me as a coach. I still believe I have a better chance of winning a game if I am coaching a team that plays together as a unit and executes a game plan, as opposed to coaching a superior group of athletes that don't come together on the same page.

My fun on the handball and paddleball courts didn't stop me from yearning to play basketball. Again, this desire was not fueled by a love of the game. I refuse to be mistreated by people. When I get smacked down by life, I make it my mission to go out and prove that I am capable of doing anything. In this instance, I was getting an unfair shake on the basketball courts of New York City because I was short. I refused to accept this and I never would. When groups of kids would think they had an easy target and pick on me for being short, I would fight the biggest kid they had. I couldn't fight them all so I figured if I went after the biggest I would get my point across. I didn't start fights, but if I had to do it to protect myself I would. I once asked a summer league coach why he didn't pick me for his team. When his answer was that I couldn't dunk a ball, dunking became my mission. I went to the "bitty baskets" at the elementary schools. The rims there were six feet high. After mastering the ball placement element of the dunk, I combined it with the jumping part and in a matter of time I could do it at will. I had a football player's lower body, thick calves and thighs, and although some people were shocked that someone 5'6'' could dunk, I was not.

When the winter of 1958 came, I still had not played a single pick up game on the courts of the New York. Christmas that year would be the beginning of my eventual basketball life. My mother got me a ball for $1.99. For that price, it was nothing fancy. It weighed less than a regulation ball but I still cherished it. My mother worked so hard and I knew that this was the best she could do. She did not get me the ball because she saw in me skill that would lead to great things. I think she had two main reasons, in addition to my happiness, for the gift. There was a playground directly next door to our apartment building. If I was there with my new ball, she could go to the window, yell out "Willie James" and have me back inside immediately. She was at work so much that I think the second reason was even more of her motive. In her mind, basketball was a sport for big men. If I played basketball and I had big friends, they would be able to protect her undersized son. I didn't have a babysitter. Playing ball in the nearby park would be my babysitter. Playing ball with my new giant friends would be my babysitter. Her gift was a form of protection.

I did not plan on waiting for the nice weather to begin practicing. In a way, winter was the perfect time for me to start playing. There was no one else on the courts, so for once I wouldn't be turned away. Also, there would be no groups of kids around to steal the ball from me or try to start trouble.

On my first day with the ball, the court was covered with a thick layer of white and black New York City snow. No problem. I took the cover of a garbage can and trudged slowly towards the basket. I used the cover like a cookie cutter. I placed it on the ground, pressed down hard, and removed all the snow from within the outline. I created one possible space from which to move and shoot. And so it began. I would stay there for hours, day after day, working on my shot. No matter how cold it got or how much my body craved the warmth of the indoors, I refused to stop. In fact, I eventually had to cut the tips off of my gloves so I'd have the proper touch on the ball. How do you think my mother reacted when she found out I ruined my only pair of gloves to practice basketball by myself in the winter?

Back in those days, there was no three point shot in basketball. But I eventually moved my shooting spot farther and farther away from the basket. At some point I was about six feet in from the jump ball circle you see on hardwood courts. I did this for two reasons. I realized that taller defenders were going to be able to put their arms up and easily block my shots if I was in close to the basket. They might not even have to jump. So I figured that I needed to develop a good outside shot. I also knew that I would have to have an arc to my shot as a way of dealing with the height of defenders, and going far from the basket helped me develop this skill.

As I continued to practice by myself into the spring, I was noticed by a park worker named Hilton White. At 6'3," his round frame and athleticism made him an imposing figure. This meeting would change my life forever. Hilton observed my moves, my cuts, my shots, and saw in me a player with great potential. At this point, I did not know any of the rules of basketball. All I focused on is what I could do with my ball, the rim and backboard. He taught me about the three second rule involving defenders. He taught me about the ten second rule which forces teams to cross half court in the allotted time. He taught me the names of things I was already doing—jump shot, hook shot, layup, bounce pass, two handed bounce pass, hook pass. It would have been impossible for me to eventually play organized basketball without all this knowledge.

Hilton worked with the A.A.U., the Amateur Athletic Union, which was a non-profit sports organization. He tried to take young black people, like me, and use the discipline of sports as a bridge to a better future. He also coached Nevil Shed and Willie Cager, two of my college teammates and life long friends, as well as basketball Hall of Famer Nate "Tiny" Archibald -- also a life long friend. When he died, a park on Cauldwell Avenue between 161st and 163rd street was renamed the Hilton White Playground to honor his activism. Hilton was a true hero of the community.

Hilton recruited me onto the Bronx Falcons summer league team, and this was a great experience. We would jump on the "Iron Horse," what we called the subway, and travel to every borough of the city competing against other teams. My mother would work late cleaning boarding houses in the city, and I never gave her the full flavor of how far I was traveling for games. Since the parks at that time didn't have streetlights, we played during the day and I could be home before it got too late.

Paul Lawrence Dunbar Junior High School was located on Cauldwell Avenue and 163rd Street. It was a seventh though ninth grade building. I didn't try out for the basketball team my first two years there, but my final year I felt that I had the skills needed to give it a go. In reality, it was the first time I tried out for a team-- and I made it. I was still very rough around the edges. I was the fastest player on the team, but sometimes I would outrun the ball. My shot was not perfected yet and I still had plenty of elements of my game that needed improvement. Professional sports, at the time, were not what they are today. Today, N.B.A stars like Kobe and Lebron probably have year round trainers working with them. Back then, pros would come to local school courts to shoot around, run, and do various exercises to stay in shape. I would sit there, between 5 and 7 P.M. just watching them do their thing. There was one player who towered over the rest of them. At 7'1,'' he was the most mountain of a man I had ever seen. It was Wilt Chamberlain, eventual two-time N.B.A champion and Hall of Famer. If you told me at the time that someday, after graduating college, that I would be on the court competing against him, I would have never believed you.

When I entered DeWitt Clinton High School for my sophomore year, it was once again time to try out for the school team. Again, I made it. However, I wasn't as happy as I was when I made the team in junior high. Coach Hank Jacobson told me that I would be the team's 7th man, meaning I wouldn't start. I would still get playing time, but it would be coming off the bench. I quit the team.

Coach Jacobson tried to talk me out of my decision. He told me this might hurt my chances junior year of even making the team, but I didn't listen. I returned to Hilton White and played rec-league ball instead. Now, as a coach, I would definitely discourage a player from doing what I did. I would tell the young man that being 7th on the team is better than 10th and that all the experience would pay off in the long run, but the young me would have none of it. I was motivated to improve my game and disprove any doubters. Again, I took my lack of starting as an unfair shake. I have to give Coach Jacobson credit. When I tried out again junior year he didn't hold a grudge. I was named a co-captain, and I went on to lead the team in scoring.

My junior year at Dewitt Clinton had a profound influence on my life, although I didn't realize it at the time. Our team was undefeated. We made it to the New York City high school championship game and for a place where basketball is a religion this is a very big deal. Our opponents were the Kangaroos of Boys High School in Brooklyn. They were appropriately named as they could jump higher than any team we played against all season.

The game took place at the old Madison Square Garden, at the time located on Eighth Avenue between 49th and 50th street. A few years earlier I had never played basketball before, and now I was being introduced as a starter in the "World's Most Famous Arena." I will never forget hearing my name said over the speakers. Think of it this way -- after famed Yankee

Stadium P.A. announcer Bob Sheppard retired, Derek Jeter requested that a tape of Sheppard's introduction be played for the rest of his professional home at bats. If hearing your name announced can mean that much to someone of Jeter's stature, imagine what it meant to a kid like me. The arena was sold out. There were 20,000 people there to see the outcome. I think I would have been more intimidated by the environment if I could look out and see that many faces. However, back then people were allowed to smoke cigarettes in public. From the court, I could only see the first few rows.

The game was a battle. Both teams hit shots. Both teams missed shots. There were fouls, scoring runs, high and lows on both sides-- the beauty of basketball. With the game clock winding down in the fourth quarter, I had the ball. The score was tied at 40-40. I imagine that if a movie director was working this scene, he or she would show me looking around for a player to pass to before deciding no one was open -- forcing me to take the final shot. But that's not what happened. Passing the ball never crossed my mind. I promise I was not a selfish player. As a coach, I preach to my players to do what I did in my playing days -- do whatever it takes to make your team better. But I was a scorer. Trying to score is what I did. BAM....BAM.... I moved one way and forced my way around the first defender. Vaughn Hopper, a defender who would later go on to play college ball at Syracuse, as well as find success as velvet voiced DJ on a famous Black radio station, collapsed down on me to help his teammate. But it was too late. ESPN loves to show highlights of long distance shots that win games, but lay ups count just the same. I got the ball over Hopper's arms and it went in. The buzzer echoed throughout the Garden and we won. Fans stormed the court and the first hug I got not from a teammate was from Gene, my future brother- in-law. My mother was working.

After the game, there was a ceremony and trophies were handed out. I was named to the All-Tournament team and M.V.P. of the championship game. And oddly, the significance of all of this did not hit me right away. DeWitt Clinton always had champions. We had football championships, fencing championships, and chess championships. We had a winning way at Clinton. However, when an article about the game ran in the newspaper and people started approaching me at school I finally realized that this was a big deal.

There are eight million people in New York City and I figure at least half of them play basketball. In addition to the tournament success, I was named All-City. When you combine the success I was having on the court with the good grades I was getting in the classroom, where I was working just as hard, I was almost guaranteed a scholarship to college. However, when junior year ended it still had not for one single, solitary moment entered my mind that I would go to college. No one in my family had before and I never considered what would eventually happen. I would be the first.

I looked at my basketball success junior year as a social opportunity. I showed up at the basketball courts in my neighborhood, where I had been rejected years earlier. I still, because of my height, had never been picked to play in one of the pick-up games. But now people heard of me. In the city championship, I made a name for myself. "Chico," you pick a team. Some people in the area called me Chico, which in Spanish, besides meaning boy or child, can signify something small. Not only was I now picked, I was given the honor of picking my own squad. I don't remember the name of the first person I took, but I can describe him to you. He was standing behind the fence; he did not look like the best athlete on the block, and, besides me, was the shortest person there. No one had ever picked him before.

Chapter 4: The Staircase

"Faith is taking the first step even when you don't see the whole staircase."
Dr. Martin Luther King Jr.

When you are a ten-year-old boy who has to cross a highway to get to school, you learn at an early age to deal with fear. When you move to a tough section of the Bronx, where there are gang wars and battles happening all around you, you learn to deal with fear. When you are living in a country where someone might want to physically or verbally abuse you because of the color of your skin, you learn to deal with fear. I was never in a position to let fear control my life. If I did, I could not have gotten by. However, on July 20th, 1964, just two weeks after getting married, I boarded an airplane for the first time. Unless you count someone 5'6'' dunking a basketball, I had never left the ground. And for one of the few times in my young life, fear was winning the battle.

I had decided to attend Texas Western College in El Paso. I am still not a fan of flying, and if I had my way back then I would have done anything possible to get to school another way. I looked into taking a bus, but if I had I think it would have taken me four years to get there as opposed to four years to get a degree. My bus trip from Virginia to New York, when I followed my mother's instructions and didn't move a muscle, made me realize this was just not practical. So after exploring all realistic options, I finally went to the airport with the ticket that Texas Western sent to the Bronx for me.

I will never forget the feeling I had as the passengers sat on the runway waiting for takeoff. I had a bag of luggage on my lap and my hands were digging into the arm rests. We weren't moving and I was already holding on for dear life. If I ever held a basketball this tightly it would have popped in my hands. Luckily for me, an act of kindness happened that has stayed with me forever. Fate had placed my "Airplane Mother" next to me.

"Airplane Mother" was originally from Brooklyn and was returning from a New York visit to her new home in El Paso. She was in her early forties with hair that was already showing signs of gray. She was very petite, like my mother Julia, and had as warm a smile as I have ever seen. In addition to all the physical features I have mentioned, "Airplane Mother" was white. So I was caught off guard when she put her hand on mine, told me that she could tell that I had never flown before, and promised me that everything would be just fine.

I'm not implying that I had never had a good relationship with a white person before this event. I had. But in the 1960's, for a white woman to so kindly embrace a black teenager, a complete stranger, was not something that happened a lot. I don't know if I could have made it through this flight without her. The first thing she did was tell me to put my luggage in the overhead compartment. Having never flown before, if she didn't tell me what to do my bag might have remained on my lap until I hit Texas. Next, she offered to switch seats with me so I could look out the window during the flight. She explained that during her first plane flight, looking out the window actually helped to calm her. She said it took away some of the claustrophobia that comes with being on an airplane. She told me that my ears might pop because of the altitude, so she gave me some gum to chew and told me this would help. As we taxied down the runway, she held my hand as tightly as I had held the seats. In telling this story over the years, I have always used the term "Airplane Mother" because she really was doing what my mother would have done if she were there. She protected me. For someone taking a symbolic first step in life without seeing the whole staircase, these gestures were invaluable. I knew in my heart that if the people of El Paso, black or white, were half as nice as this woman then everything would work out for me.

It is about a five hour flight from New York City to El Paso. As I stared out the window, I had a lot of time to reflect on the events of the previous year that led to me being on this plane. I guess I was thinking about my personal history, not realizing that I was headed towards making history.

By the summer of 1963, I had become a mainstay of the hugely competitive basketball courts of New York City. My habit of picking players for my team who might have been turned away by others did more than just right an injustice that had been done to me. It made me a better player. If I played with weaker players as teammates, it forced me to elevate my game. My legacy as a successful court player was starting to grow.

I found myself traveling to parks all around the city to get into games. I might jump on the subway and head down to 127th Street and Amsterdam Avenue, or walk across the Bronx over to Third Avenue looking for a game. It was a point of pride. For someone who had been kept out of this exclusive club, I loved enhancing my playground reputation. The elder statesmen of the courts, men in their thirties, called kids like me the "young bucks." We were trying to, just like they did at some point, make it on what we considered the biggest stage in the world.

New York City court players all speak the same lingo. Sports was our life. And on any court there could be a variation of the same pipe dream. For some, it was to make it as a pro. Others wanted to use basketball to go to college. There were even players that just needed to be better than the previous local legend or baller from down the block. We were all looking for

"It." Anyone who has ever played in the city playgrounds has heard the term "It." He has "It." He will never have "It." "It" was that indefinable quality that sets you apart from others. I think young people today call it the "X" factor. And if you didn't have "It," your dreams would just remain dreams.

I didn't realize it at the time, but all my experiences on the playgrounds would not only help me during my high school senior year season, but it would help me playing college ball as well. Each borough of New York has its own style of play. Brooklyn is hard-nosed defense and physical. I would go to Brooklyn, and the other boroughs, because I wanted to compete against the best in the city. I had several successful games there. However, because of my M.V.P game junior year against Boys High School, I wasn't always welcome. A friend and I once had to hightail it from the court to the subway to avoid a fight that would have seen us heavily outnumbered. The style on the Manhattan courts is "Shakin and Bakin." Players there tend to show off their dribbling and dunking skills. There is also a ton of trash talk in Manhattan. I played against guys who talked a lot while saying nothing. I think my home courts of The Bronx featured a blend of the other boroughs. We'd call our style "Basic" with a little "Flash" and plenty of "It."

Getting to play against all these styles was great, because I think there are also styles associated with different parts of the United States. Players from the Mid-West and the South tend to be shooters. This is because a lot of them play on dirt courts so dribbling properly is difficult. It's easier to pull up and shoot. West Coast players like to be smooth and laid back. They have the beach game. They glide down the court like a surfer carrying his board while trying to impress the ladies. The Northeast players are about ball handling. You can't have "It" without being a ball handler. By the time I hit Texas Western, I had been trained to handle any style you could throw at me.

Just like life, my senior year basketball season at Dewitt Clinton was fiiled with highs and lows. I remember an exciting victory we had against James Monroe High School. It was a back and forth battle between the teams, with a big individual battle between me and their best player, Ed Kranepool. Ed was a great left-handed shot and every time he put the ball in the air, it seemed to go in. He would later go on to play Major League Baseball with the New York Mets and was one of their best players through the 1970's. Another highlight of the season was a win versus Samuel Gompers. We were trailing by sixteen points at halftime. I took over the second half and we pulled it out. Since my friends and future brothers-in-law, Donald and Gene, attended Gompers, I got the family bragging rights. It was fun to tease them about that game.

The low light of the season came against our rivals, Boys High School from Brooklyn. They beat us in the semi-finals, avenging their loss from my M.V.P. Championship game at Madison Square Garden. This was my only loss as a high school player. In my two years playing for DeWitt Clinton, we went 38-1. But any real athlete will tell you that you always want to win the final game of the season. To this day, that loss bothers me. I take losing personally. I have never been a good loser and I hope I never will be. Don't mistake getting sore at losing with being a sore loser. As a player and now coach, I demand good sportsmanship. In the hundreds of games I have participated in as a player and coach, I have never received a technical foul from a referee -- although I will admit once or twice I was close. After a game, alone, I will dwell on a loss and replay in my head what I could have done differently to change the outcome in my team's favor. As the best player on the team, I felt it was my responsibility to make us win that game. Basketball is a team sport and I am a "team first" man. With all the individual accomplishments that I had senior year, I still look back at that season with regret and a sense of failure.

I was the leading scorer for my team my last year, and it's possible that I was the leading scorer in all of New York City. These individual numbers, combined with the overall success of the DeWitt Clinton team during my time there, led to me being named a 1964 High School All-American. For a high school player, there is no higher individual honor. There were some notable high school players to be named All-American that year. Wes Unseld went on to play for the Baltimore Bullets. He was the 1969 N.B.A Rookie of the Year and also won the N.B.A. M.V.P that season. The only other person to ever accomplish this feat was the person I'd watch practice in my high school gym years earlier, Wilt Chamberlain. Butch Beard eventually played over ten N.B.A seasons and coached in the league as well. Ironically, both of these players refused to play college ball at Kentucky, a school that I would eventually be linked to forever.

The most notable All-American that year was a fellow New Yorker. He attended a private school in Manhattan called Power Memorial High School. His name was Lew Alcindor. After converting to Islam, he changed his name to what most people now know him as -- Kareem Abdul-Jabbar. Kareem is the all-time leading scorer in N.B.A history and arguably the best player the league has ever seen. I remember several articles about the All-American team that year that mentioned me and Lew Alcindor in the same paragraph. At 7'2," he was the tallest person named All-American. At 5'6,"I was the shortest.

As a basketball coach at Spring Valley High School, one of my responsibilities is to help players with the college process. But I am not the only one doing this. It is a school-wide effort. I have seen our principal, assistant principals, guidance department, and teachers from all subjects work with students to help get them into college. We have a college week with representatives from dozens of schools telling our students what they need to do. By the time one of our roughly 1100 students is a senior, they have received a lot of individual attention to address their future education. This was not the case for me at DeWitt Clinton.

There were close to 6,000 students attending DeWitt Clinton by the time I was a senior. Our Guidance Department was overloaded, and there were too many of us for them to be hands on the way it is at Spring Valley. You might think that they would go out of their way to help a stand out athlete like me, but the school was filled with stand outs in academics, arts, and of course, sports. For example, John Carlos, a track star at my school, along with Tommie Smith, would become famous for making the 'Black Power' salute at the 1968 Summer Olympics. We had eventual Olympians! My accomplishments on the court were not the school's number one priority, as much as I appreciated being a student there.

Mr. Katz, my English teacher, was in his late 60's. He had plenty of thick gray hair and was probably one of the few people at the school who was shorter than me. If it were not for him, I probably would have never attended college. He took an interest in Willie Worsley the person and student, not just Willie Worsley the basketball player. For all the coaches I have had as an athlete, Mr. Katz was my academic coach.

When you grow up in poverty, long term plans like college do not cross your mind. The things that cross your mind are surviving until the next day. Everything is day to day. You worry about food, clothes -- the nuts and bolts of existence. Mr. Katz helped me change my way of thinking. He saw for me "a staircase" that I didn't know existed.

At that point, if you had said S.A.T. to me I might have thought you were asking me about my plans for Saturday night. I didn't know about applications, scholarships, financial aid, or any other element of the process. Why would I? No one had ever mentioned any of these things to me before. Since my mother and I were just trying to make ends meet, I planned on getting my diploma and looking for a job. If I could do anything to help my mother not have to work two jobs, as she had her whole life, I would be a success. Because of hard work, I had a decent grade point average. But Mr. Katz thought I needed to work on my S.A.T. score.

Just like I would do if it were basketball, I stayed after school and worked on my game. Mr. Katz gave me books to read and we would talk about them, more like friends than teacher and student. We might sit by the window with our feet propped up and study while looking out at the Bronx below us. This relaxed atmosphere really helped. I didn't look at this as a chore. When we first started, I was such a nervous test-taker that I actually stressed about getting a zero. Mr. Katz gently laughing and telling me that was impossible helped me with my jitters. As I can tell you from my life in sports, confidence is greatly linked with success and he was helping me feel better about my chances on the exam. My score definitely improved because of all the vocabulary prep work he did with me.

In 1964, our country was fighting the Vietnam War. High school students who did not enroll in college were immediately eligible for the draft. Going to Vietnam was not something I was interested in doing. I had seen many people in my neighborhood get drafted. Many of them never returned and the ones who did seemed much worse off from when they left. Even people who enlisted, with the hopes of gaining skills for future employment, returned right back into a life of poverty. Going to war would not enable me to take care of my single mother or future family. However, a college education would give me a chance at a career -- something I had never thought possible.

As a high school All-American, I started to receive attention from colleges all over the country. The first step in the process is a letter of interest. It is basically a questionnaire that the schools ask you to fill out. This is a non-binding agreement. It is not an offer, but letters of interest often lead to official offers and scholarships. Usually these letters were sent to our athletic department and I would get them in unopened envelopes. Again, Mr. Katz helped me. We'd go through the letters and try to make heads or tails of the information. The University of Cincinnati sent me a letter, as did Ohio State. At the time, these schools were basketball powerhouses and I was so proud that they knew about me. I cannot describe the feeling I got when I received a letter from U.C.L.A., led by the most famous college coach and legend John Wooden. My immediate reaction was to jump at the opportunity to go there. How could I not pounce on any interest U.C.L.A. would have in me?

Mr. Katz helped me look at the decision from a different angle. He thought I'd do better as a big fish in a little pond, as opposed to a little fish in a big pond. If I went to a place like U.C.L.A., I would be just another Tom, Dick, or Harry. I could get lost in the shuffle and if I ever struggled there academically, I might not get as much support as I would at another school. The more I thought about how different life in California might be, the more I realized he was right. Mr. Katz suggested I look at schools that were building a basketball program from the ground up.

Overall, I got close to 100 letters of interest from schools across the country. However, approximately seventy-five percent of these schools backed off on their interest at some point along the way. I couldn't understand it. My grades hadn't changed. I wasn't a discipline problem at Clinton. They knew my S.A.T. scores when they sent the original letter of interest. When I would talk to Mr. Katz about this, he always seemed to have the same answer. "Willie, that is an almost all-white school." If I listed the names of every school that I suspected backed off of me because of race, this book would be two or three pages longer. But I'm not going to do that. As a coach, I still deal with these institutions all the time. I know that what happened in the 1960's is not representative of these colleges today. It was a sign of the times. Worsley is not what I consider a common black surname. Today, it is much easier for schools to research a player. An internet search could probably tell you 100 different things about a student. But back then, scouting and research was much more involved. It was a tough pill to swallow. There were schools that were interested, on paper, in a white Willie Worsley, but not interested in a black Willie Worsley with the exact same qualifications.

On November 22nd, 1963, President John F. Kennedy was assassinated. Anyone alive at that time can remember where they were when they heard the shocking news. It is one of the greatest tragedies in American history. At the time it happened, college was not on my radar. However, this event almost had a huge impact on where I'd go to school.

At first, I really didn't show my mother the letters of interest I was receiving from schools. She would not really have known the difference between one school over another. But when the Miners of Texas Western showed such strong interest in me, it was time to get her involved with the process. I really looked at Texas Western as a good fit for me. It was a small school, with enrollment around 2,000 students. Local schools like N.Y.U. and St. Johns had much higher enrollments. Also, there was a part of me that liked the idea of leaving New York. Maybe college would be my only real chance to see the world. Texas Western was offering me a full, four year scholarship. How could I pass that up?

My mother had always put a lot of trust in me. She knew I had to be a man at a young age. She looked at me as a level-headed person with very good instincts. But in her mind, because President Kennedy was killed in Dallas, that meant that Dallas was a dangerous place. It was certainly too dangerous for her only child. I tried to explain to her the enormity of the state of Texas. Dallas and El Paso are 638 miles apart. It takes about eleven hours to travel from one city to the other by car. In reality, it would have been a shorter car ride from our Bronx apartment to Toronto, Canada. Stories like this did not seem to sway her. If the president could get killed in Dallas, anyone could. Luckily for me, Texas Western did have something in my mother's eyes that offered her baby a form of protection.

My childhood friends, and former Bronx Falcons teammates Willie "Scoops" Cager and Nevil "Butch" Shed, were already attending Texas Western. They were both a little older than me and their paths led them to El Paso. There has been a lot written over the years about exactly how Don Haskins came to recruit me, and here is my take. The school was interested in me because of my abilities and my standing as a high school All-American. When Coach Haskins found out where I was from, he made the connection with Willie and Nevil and both of my friends put in a good word for me. Years earlier, Hilton White, who made a life helping local kids, used his great reputation to connect both Willie and Nevil with Coach Haskins. Coach called Hilton to check on me, and he was told that my size would not be an issue. Just as he had done years earlier by teaching me the rules of basketball, Hilton White was still having a positive influence on my life. Coach Haskins was assured that my status as an All-American was legit and I could play with anyone. None of this would have mattered except for one thing. Willie Cager is 6'6" and Nevil Shed is 6'8." Even though my mother thought Dallas was a dangerous neighboring town to El Paso, she loved the idea of me already having big friends there. Her motivation years earlier with the basketball Christmas gift was for me to get protected by big friends. I think she looked at this as divine intervention and gave me her blessing.

It's important to realize something about my ability to attend Texas Western. I would not have been able to go if it weren't for my wife of fifty years, Claudia. She is one of the most amazing people in the world. Claudia is a driving force behind any success I have ever had.

Claudia and I knew each other since we were thirteen years old. As I mentioned earlier, I befriended her brothers on the playground and eventually became close with all her siblings. By the time we were fifteen, it was just us. We were finally old enough to have real romance and we have ever since. She has always been a beautiful woman. I was instantly attracted to her dark brown skin and eyes, wonderful smile, and long gorgeous legs. She was also a great athlete. Some of our first dates were at the handball court, where I met Donald and Gene. To hear her tell it, she is the best handball player in the family. For the purposes of this book, I will not dispute this title. She always called me her "country pumpkin." That is because, as a person from the South, I was always wearing loud colors. It was not uncommon for me to wear -- in my mind very stylish -- bright orange pants and shirts.

Claudia always tells it like it is. She doesn't just tell me what I want to hear and that has always worked towards improving our overall family situation. She makes me a better person. For example, I hate change. Knowing this, Claudia puts her magical spin on things and forces me to deal with change in a way that I can handle. Claudia is as smart as can be. She skipped a grade in elementary school, so even though I am a week older than she is, she graduated high school a year earlier than I did. I think she would have made a great lawyer, but I was the one who got to go to college. There has always been a big part of me that has felt that Claudia, with her brains, should have gotten this opportunity. However, in the 1960's the idea of women attending college was not what it is today.

There was another reason, besides the role of women in the 1960's, that kept Claudia from going to college. It was her maternal instinct. In the spring of 1964, we found out that Claudia was pregnant. Since we were fifteen, we always knew we'd get married. This only sped up the process a little bit. Our families were very happy. As an only child, having Donald, Gene, Teresa and Dolores in my life has been amazing. They were like my own brothers and sisters. Claudia's father, Gene Reinhart, always liked me. Even before we got married he treated me like his own son and he did so his entire life. I was already a part of Claudia's family.

When my mother Julia took me, at eleven years old, to enroll in junior high school, I found out something I never knew before. It said Willie Worsley on my birth certificate, and not Willie Buck. It's possible my parents didn't get married until after I was born. I'm not really sure. But I was shocked. My mother always loved my father so much that maybe she never told me this because she didn't want to, in her mind, disrespect him. After eleven years thinking I was Willie Buck, I became Willie Worsley. And I think this also contributed to our desire to get married before I left for school. We wanted to break a negative stereotype of a young black family with different last names. I was raised in a single parent household. Claudia's mother died at an early age, so Claudia was raised by her father and older siblings. We were going to make our situation work. We were going to provide our children with a two parent, stable household, and nothing was going to stop us. And since we've been married for fifty years, I think we have been very successful.

There is no way I could have left my mother all alone in New York City to attend college. I would never have done that. Claudia volunteered to move in with my mother. Since Claudia's family lived in the same building as my mother and me, she packed up her stuff and made the big move -- fourteen flights up. My mother and Claudia always got along overall, but I still consider this an amazing sacrifice on Claudia's part. I've always believed that you can't have two women in charge of one kitchen. I'm sure it would not be easy for most people to live with their in-law and because El Paso was so far away, I could not travel home that often. And to this day, as our family has expanded from children, to married children, to grandchildren -- Claudia is the anchor that has kept our family's ship steady for the duration of any storm we've faced.

In 2006, Walt Disney Pictures released the film *Glory Road*. The movie depicts the events that led to the 1966 N.C.A.A. Basketball Championship game between Kentucky and Texas Western -- a game in which I played. There were premieres in some of the major markets in the country, but I decided to attend the one in El Paso, Texas. How could I resist returning to my home away from home to see myself portrayed in a major motion picture? As I was standing, facing the screen before the movie started, I heard a voice say, "Hello, my baby." When I turned around, I saw a woman in her eighties whose warm smile I recognized immediately. It was my "Airplane Mother." She was in a wheelchair, but still made it to the premiere. The emotion I felt seeing her was so strong that I welled up with tears, something I am not a fan of doing in public. I offered to help her with the wheelchair, but she would have none of it. She did ask one favor of me. She asked if we could watch the movie together. I wouldn't have had it any other way. I got an aisle seat, with her by my side, and we held hands -- just like we did during my first airplane flight decades earlier. Together, we shared tears of joy and reminisced about the staircases of our lives.

Chapter 5: Iron Head

"A man is at his youngest when he thinks he is a man, not yet realizing that his actions must show it." Mary Renault, *The King Must Die*

If you asked me at eighteen if I was a man, I'm sure I would have confidently laughed off the question. Of course I was. I had always felt that I became a man at a young age. At ten, I was taking care of myself while my mother worked two jobs. When we moved to New York, I survived life in the tough Harlem neighborhoods. I was a High School All- American for Dewitt Clinton and a star on the elite courts of New York City. Only a man could accomplish these things. However, I now realize that I did not really become a man until after I finished my first season for the Texas Miners of El Paso. And as much as basketball has been a huge part of my life, it is not what made me a man. It was something else much more important.

When my plane landed on Texas soil, I'm sure I thanked God for getting me there safely. It was not an easy first flight. When I tried to thank "Airplane Mother" for getting me through it all, she refused to say goodbye. What good mother would leave her child alone in an airport when he had no idea what to do next? She walked me to the baggage claim and helped me find my things. If she hadn't, I'm sure the little bit of luggage I had somehow managed to check in back in New York would still be there going around in circles on the conveyor belt. Then, she waited until someone from the school came to get me. When someone finally arrived, we said goodbye but it wasn't a sad permanent goodbye. She promised to check in on me, and there were many times in my years playing at El Paso when I'd look in the stands and see her there with her family cheering me on. What an amazing woman!

I'm sure that for most people, the first day of college involves settling in to the new surroundings. Some probably walk around campus; while others hang up posters in their room trying to send out signals to strangers about what they think is cool and interesting. I was taken straight to the gym. I didn't see my room. I wasn't given a tour of the campus. I still had my luggage with me while I listened to the squeak of sneakers on the Texas Western courts. For some, this might have been unsettling. I loved it. The courts were always my home away from home. This also sent me a message. They were serious about basketball and I needed to take it seriously too. This first moment on campus set a tone for my years there as a player.

Within forty-eight hours of arriving in Texas, I was interviewed by a local newspaper and a television station. I would not play my first collegiate game for another three months, but the media was already interested. Amateur sports are hugely popular in Texas. That television interview taught me a lesson that has stayed with me forever. Always follow the "red dot." Don't look at the interviewer, or cameraman, or the people in the background -- if you look at the red dot on the camera, you will be looking the audience at home right in the eye. The newspaper reporters were interested in me because I was an All-American. Part of me felt like they thought I was involved in some sinister plot. "Did this guy kill the real Willie Worsley and steal his identity? There is no way someone 5'6" is going to come here and be a star. There must be a mistake. Is this an episode of Candid Camera?" They had heard the name Willie Worsley, but knew nothing else about me. I wasn't nervous being interviewed, but I was surprised at all the attention I was receiving. I think part of it had to do with the fact that I was coming from New York City. There was a curiosity about me.

    I was in El Paso in July because I needed to take two preliminary courses and receive at least a B in each to be academically eligible for N.C.A.A. basketball and receive my scholarship. I would not meet, or reunite, with any of my teammates for months. This created an unusual living situation. Since athletes were given their own dorms, and I was the only athlete there for the summer, I had an entire floor to myself. Some people might like this, but I hated it. I was lonely. In New York City, even when you are alone, you have fire alarms, honking horns, subway cars, buses, and people on the street cursing at each other to keep you company. Here, I found myself in bed staring at the ceiling and praying for the quiet to end.

    Because it was the summer and I was the only player on campus, I had to look for pickup games to keep myself in shape. Running and exercising was good, but I also wanted to keep my game moves sharp. The N.C.A.A. has very strict rules on the amount of hours athletes can practice, so I found myself going off campus and playing without the coaching staff knowing about it. Coming from The Bronx, I did not have a car, or even a driver's license. Why would I? In New York, you can walk or take public transportation anywhere you need to go. I had to rely on other students to help me navigate the area. I would often hitch a ride, from students of all racial backgrounds, to the nearby army base, Fort Bragg. Here, I could get into games with grown men and it was a great way for me to maintain the competitive edge I developed back home. Don't get me wrong, I did plenty of walking but these car rides contributed to a lot of special memories. My height was even a factor when hitching rides from people. A lot of cars in the 1960's had a hump in the middle of the back seats. Most cars did not have bucket seats the way they do today. When I would hitch with a few other guys, because I was the shortest passenger, they'd always try to stick me with the humped, uncomfortable middle seat. As fast as I had ever run on a basketball court, I'd find myself racing to cars, positioning myself in the window seat, and locking the door so I couldn't be pushed towards the middle.

I wanted to leave New York to see the world, and now I was taking trips to places like Albuquerque, New Mexico and Tucson, Arizona. I loved these new experiences. I will never forget looking out over the Grand Canyon. The enormity of it probably has an impact on anyone who has ever been there, but for someone who grew up in an apartment without a bathroom I could not believe what I was seeing.

Henry Iba was elected to the Naismith Basketball Hall of Fame in 1969. He won two gold medals as a coach in the 1960's, and many Americans feel he was robbed of a third. He was involved in one of the most controversial games in basketball history. In the 1972 Olympics, the officials made several late game calls involving the clock that gave the Russians the Gold Medal. Besides his Olympic success, Iba had a successful run at Oklahoma State University. Don Haskins, my eventual head coach and hall of famer, played for Henry Iba at Oklahoma. So when Coach Haskins needed an assistant coach, he picked Moe Iba, son of the legendary Henry Iba. The coaching tree in sports is special. There is a beauty to coaches wanting to pass on what they've learned to people they care about. Henry Iba passed down his expertise to Coach Haskins and Moe Iba, and I have tried to do the same now as a varsity coach. Tony Wooten, the father of three of my granddaughters, is my assistant coach. He is like a son to me and I try to treat him that way, just like Claudia's father did when I was a young man.

My first meeting with Coach Haskins was memorable, but brief. He shook my hand and asked me questions about Willie Worsley the person, not Willie Worsley the player. He asked about my transition to El Paso and how I was adapting to my new surroundings. He also stressed to me the importance of going to classes and maintaining my grades. Unlike what many people wrote about Texas Western after March 19, 1966, education was a priority for the players. He never once mentioned basketball.

Coach Haskins was about 6'2" and in his mid-thirties when we first met. You could still see the college athlete in him, even though he developed what I like to call a "coach's belly." But it wasn't anything physical that made him intimidating, it was his pure intensity. Intimidation can only work for so long before it loses its effect. But he combined intimidation with a necessary ingredient – he was fair. And because of that, you could be afraid of him, but be willing to follow his lead. He had an amazing bag of tricks in his arsenal. There is an image that I think most people have of sports coaches screaming at their players to get results. He would do that, sure. But he could also intimidate by standing at the foul line and shooting baskets with his eyes closed. It was amazing to see shot after shot go in. How could we argue with someone who could do that? As a coach, I have borrowed that move. It is one of many coaching strategies that I credit to the influence of Don Haskins

I was happy when the fall of 1964 arrived. I passed my summer classes. I was moved from my solitary dorm to Burgess Hall so I would be with the rest of the basketball team. My freshman roommate was Willie Cager. I always wondered if they put us together because we were friends with similar backgrounds, or that if they ever needed one of us they could just send someone to Willie's room and have a 50/50 chance of finding the right guy. Unlike what people might think about the 1960's, the dorms were not segregated by race. Black and white athletes lived in the same dorm and I made new black and white friends each day.

The college basketball season doesn't start until October, so before I ever stepped on a court for a real game I stepped into classrooms to begin my education. The school created my schedule. I took an education class in a building located between my dorm and the gym. There were times I felt like I was sneaking to class because I didn't want Coach Haskins to see me. I wanted him to think of me positively, but not think of me often. I was afraid that if he saw me, he might pull me into the gym to run laps just for the hell of it. I took a required English 101, which was more like a speech class. For me, this was a nightmare. I have heard of a famous survey where they ask people to write down what they are most afraid of. Public speaking always comes in first and death finishes a distant second. I can understand that. Between my introverted personality and the speech impediment I had at the time, getting up in front of sixty strangers in an auditorium and doing oral interpretations was not my cup of tea. A third class I had was Metaling, and it was on Saturday mornings at 8 A.M. We were, after all, the Miners of Texas Western. The school taught people how to work in mines so, in this class, I learned about rocks and minerals. It was the equivalent of an earth science class. Over time, I realized why they gave me this elective. The school, or coaches, hoped that an early Saturday class would keep me, as an athlete, from staying out too late on Friday night.

Juarez, Mexico is less than a half an hour away from El Paso, Texas. There is an old joke in El Paso that goes, "It costs three cents to cross the bridge into Juarez, and five cents to cross it on the way home." It was common for Texas Western students, including my teammates, to make the trip to Juarez. Some were looking to drink or meet girls, but I was married and not a drinker so those motives were of no interest to me. After going to Juarez once or twice, I never really felt the need to go back. Juarez did offer cheap gifts and that was something I took advantage of. I was able to buy leather coats, cowboy boots, and pocketbooks for Claudia and my mother and send them home for Christmas. They cost a fraction of what they would have in the United States.

I was struggling with my classes freshman year. In high school, a student goes to class every day. In college, you went three times a week. I was not adjusting to budgeting my time. The scheduling of college courses made it easy for me to procrastinate. Having days in between classes always made me feel like I could do my work tomorrow. Then tomorrow would come and I'd see another tomorrow and it started a bad cycle. I was never one to ask people for help. When Hilton White saw me on the playground, he approached me with help. When Mr. Katz tutored me at Dewitt Clinton, it was his idea. Even now, asking for help is not easy for me. I accept help, but it's tough for me to seek it out. But in my freshman year, I knew that I needed help or I would not get by. Since my first conversation with Coach Haskins involved school work, I knew this was important.

    I approached some of my teammates for advice. How would you do this? How would you do that? It worked. I improved my study habits. When I would get home from class, I would review all my notes while the lecture was fresh in my mind. If I had five chapters to read, I wouldn't wait until the last minute to do it. I would break it up over time and give myself time to re-read it if necessary. I found that starting with the work I wanted to do the least was a good style for me. It stopped the study stress from lingering in my mind. Even now, if I have chores that I need to do I start with the one I like the least. If I don't feel like taking out the garbage, that's first on my list. I passed all of my freshman year courses, but school work didn't come as naturally to me as basketball did.

    Moe Iba had a huge influence on my success at Texas Western, and for that I owe him a great deal. At 5'10' with short, black cropped hair and a squeaky voice, similar to Coach Haskins, it was not his physical presence that commanded people's respect. But he was a good person with a superior knowledge of the game passed down to him from his coaching legend father. Moe's left shoulder slanted down lower than his right, but this did not hinder his ability on the court. He could shoot a basketball as well as anyone I had ever seen. Moe liked me. He was a quiet, stick to himself type of guy and he saw similar qualities in me. Moe took me under his wing and tried to help me make the social transition to school. He always made me feel as though I had someone to talk to about life, not just basketball, if I ever needed it. Moe helped me emerge from my cocoon a little bit and I think my college experience was better because of his help.

    On the court, Moe Iba helped me become the player I needed to be if I was going to see minutes from Coach Haskins. Back then, the N.C.A.A. forced schools to have a freshman team and a varsity team. If you were a freshman, you were ineligible to play varsity until sophomore year. I was not a fan of this at all. I was ready for the big games as soon I arrived. The rationale was that it gave players, young players, an extra year to grow and mature. Moe Iba was Don Haskin's assistant on the varsity bench, but he served in a dual role as head coach of the freshman team.

    Texas Western Public Relations Director Ed Mullins loved to create nicknames for the players. David 'Big Daddy D" and Nevil "The Shadow" Shed were his creations. He was also responsible for my nickname – "Iron

Head." I was called this because at times I could be stubborn as a mule and would often butt heads with coaches and teammates.

If you asked Coach Haskins the three keys to winning basketball, his answer would have been: 1) Defense 2) Defense 3) Defense. Coach Iba and Haskins were constantly analyzing the play of the freshman team to see who would make varsity the next year. This decision was huge. It let them know how many players to recruit and at what positions. Putting together a team was like completing a jigsaw puzzle with pieces from all over the country. Moe knew that if I was going to make it on varsity, I needed to become a defender and, at that point, I couldn't guard a telephone pole. Since I want my grandchildren to read this book, I can't print the words Moe Iba would scream at me to describe my defense. And when he did, I would glare at him. I'd roll my eyes. My face would contort from anger. What I didn't realize was that Coach Iba was making me a better all-around player. If I knew in 1964 what I would realize after our success in 1966, I would have put more effort into my defensive play. Defense wins championships.

At Dewitt Clinton High School, we would play zone defense. I was encouraged to steal the ball and score points on a fast break. On the courts of New York City, the defensive scheme is, "Hurry up and shoot so you can get the ball back and score again." I was an All-American, and you didn't become and All-American by playing defense. Shooters and scorers became All-Americans. So when Moe Iba taught me how to play the man-to-man system employed by Coach Haskins, it was almost like I was learning the game for the first time again – similar to when Hilton White mentored me years earlier.

The freshman team went 18-2, and I don't really remember our two losses. We were a good squad. I was one of the five starters, and the bench players rarely saw any time on the court. David Palasio was a small forward from El Paso. He was already a good defender, as well as strong ball handler. Tony Harper was also an El Paso local. He was a heady player. He was basketball smart and was always in the right place at the right time. My long time friend and roommate Willie Cager also started. I already knew what he could do. He was a snake on the court, with the ability to slither his way into an opening and create space for himself.

At 6'7" and 245 pounds, David Lattin was a monster of a man. If it were not for the rule prohibiting it, he would have been starting for the varsity team. He was as strong as an ox. He didn't drink or smoke, and really took care of his body. David's imposing build was all muscle and he probably had two or three percent body fat. A Houston native, David might have been voted one of the best dressers in the state of Texas. He was clean cut, handsome, and knew about all the latest fashions. He would make sure his pants were creased exactly the right way and his shirt didn't have a wrinkle to speak of.

David Lattin certainly saw my 'Iron Head' from time to time, and I got it back from him as well. We were brothers battling together on the same team but, at the same time we had a competitive rivalry with each other. David was the best and I wanted to be the best. And, at the same time, David saw me, someone half his size, starting for the same team. Coach Haskins had a strict policy in regards to how we taped up our ankles before games. We were all issued high top Chuck Taylor sneakers and one day I noticed that David was wearing low tops. Why did he get low tops and the rest of us high tops? I also preferred low tops, as this is what I wore in high school and on the courts of the city. My antenna went up. I have always fought back against being treated unfairly and I definitely wanted to keep up with David. I almost looked at these sneakers as a competition I lost to him and I wanted none of it. "Iron Head" went to the trainers and make a stink about the whole thing. Eventually, I was given the same sneakers as David, and in my heart I felt like I had won.

December of 1964 was simultaneously a difficult and joyous time. I could not return home for Christmas because I had no money to finance the trip. I spent my birthday, December 13th, without my family. I did not get to celebrate Claudia's birthday, on December 20th, with her. But by far the hardest thing about not being able to return home was missing the birth of my first child -- my beautiful daughter Etta May. She was born on December 15th and was named after Claudia's mother. The happiness I felt was indescribable. I was a father.

January, February, March, April, -- all these months went by and I still had not met my angel Etta. I just simply could not make it home because of my financial situation. The school flew me down, but getting home was my responsibility. I had enough money for one return trip home and I had to save that for the end of the school year. Every class, practice, dribble, shot, pass, dunk, and game of my freshman year happened before I met my daughter.

In May of 1965, I boarded a Greyhound bus and returned to the Bronx. The impractical, seemingly endless bus ride that got me seated next to "Airplane Mother" was now my only option to get home. It was wonderful to see everyone after so long. Claudia and my mother looked great and I could tell things were working out with their living situation.

Holding Etta in my arms for the first time is certainly at the top of the highlight reel of my life. If you were making a movie of my life, I could see the director having a light shining down from heaven onto Etta's face because that is how emotional I felt. When I saw her chubby cheeks, which I knew she got from me, it was a life-changing experience. It was that moment that I became a man. I realized that I left for El Paso a boy, but now I had to be a man. Children make parents realize that they cannot be selfish. I could not be "Iron Head" with my daughter. I had to open up my mind and change my attitude. I had to start to accept what other people told me. Maybe they were right. There is still a little "Iron Head" in me, but from the moment I met Etta, I looked at life differently. I knew that when I returned to El Paso, I would work on my defense or do anything else they wanted me to do. I would practice harder and study harder than I ever had before. This was no longer just about me. I needed to be a success so that my daughter could someday be a success. I had seen the Grand Canyon. Now, if Etta needed me to jump over the Grand Canyon, I would figure out a way to do it. I had to. That's what a man does and I was now a man. Etta.

Chapter 6: The Ties That Bind

"Farewell has a sweet sound of reluctance. Good-by is short and final, a word with teeth sharp to bite through the string that ties past to the future."
John Steinbeck, *The Winter of Our Discontent*

Although I wasn't the biggest fan of traveling into Mexico, there was one advantage I enjoyed by living in the neighboring city of El Paso, Texas. Whenever there was a bullfight in Juarez, I knew we would have steak for dinner in the school cafeteria. One of the adjustments college students make when going to school involves eating. At home, you can eat when you want. If you are still hungry, you might decide to have seconds. But at school, you have to show up for breakfast, lunch, and dinner when they tell you to. And after your allotment of food is dished out, that's it. Luckily for me, some of the Spanish speaking cafeteria workers took care of me. Just like in the neighborhoods of the Bronx, they gave me the nickname "Chico" and would slip me seconds whenever they could do it without getting into trouble. I started to wonder if the name Chico was tattooed on my forehead. I think they were trying to support me since we shared a common trait. We were all vertically challenged.

Home-cooked meals were certainly a bonus when I returned to The Bronx after my freshman season at Texas Western. Basketball had me in great shape, but to Claudia and my mother I looked thin. I think my mother thought I was finally losing some of my baby fat and she didn't like it. My mother would make me fried chicken, cabbage, and corn bread. The next night, Claudia might make ribs or liver with gravy. There was plenty of pork and beans, inexpensive canned foods -- like spinach and green peas, followed by a delicious dessert baked by my wife. With our roots in the South, of course my mother would make smoked neck bones and black eyed peas with white rice on the side. I went from limited amounts of food, or food secretly being slipped to me, to having two personal gourmet cooks happy to feed me like a king.

Of course, when someone says they crave a home-cooked meal, it is not really just about food. It means they are homesick, and that was definitely the case for me. I was determined to make up for lost time with Etta and take advantage of every moment I had with her over the summer of 1965. I was going to bond with my angel. I would give her so much love that there would be enough of it left over for her when I returned to school in the fall. If I hugged her enough, even when I was gone I would still be there.

When I wanted to learn how to play basketball, there were coaches like Hilton White to show me the basics. When I needed to improve in school, Mr. Katz took me under his wing and showed me what to do. But when you become a first-time parent, despite the many people telling you what you should and should not be doing, it is all on-the-job training. Being a rookie daddy was much more complicated, and rewarding, than being a rookie on any basketball team. I had no coach or handbook to guide me.

I knew that being a mother and grandmother were much tougher jobs than attending classes and putting a ball in a basket, so I was determined to give Claudia and my mother a breather for the months I was home. When Etta woke in the middle of the night, I always tried to be the one to go calm her down. Often, I would take Etta into the living room and let her sleep on my chest so Claudia could be rested for work the next day. I learned about feeding, burping, the importance of putting on a baby bonnet when outside on a sunny day – all things I had never thought about before. I always found changing Etta's diaper to be an adventure. In 1965, disposable diapers were not as common as they are today. We used cloth diapers, and that required me to use safety pins to keep them on her body. No matter how many times I did this, I was afraid to poke Etta. The process probably took five times longer than it needed to, but I loved every minute of it.

Athletes are known to be a superstitious crowd, and I certainly have some superstitions of my own. One of my biggest has nothing to do with sports. I don't like to say "goodbye." I almost look at that word as a jinx, with a horrible finality to it. I feel like it implies that I will never see a person again, and I don't like that feeling. I always tell my children and grandchildren I love them when we part, even if I know we are planning to see each other the next day. I don't take anything for granted. So when it was time for me to head back to college in the fall of 1965, I refused to say goodbye to my mother, Claudia, and Etta. I'm sure I said "take care" or "see you later," because I knew they'd always be with me. I'm going to another state, but I'm not leaving.

In addition to taking care of Etta, I did have another job during the summer of 1965. Through an anti-poverty program, designed to give young kids a chance to make minimum wage, I went to work for the New York City Housing Authority (NYCHA). I knew somebody who knew somebody and I was put in charge of teaching basketball clinics. I didn't realize it at the time, but this became my first taste of coaching basketball. Becoming a coach was not something I had ever pictured myself doing.

I always looked at being a player as a 50/50 proposition: you win the game or you lose the game. But I didn't feel that way about coaching because even the winning coach had to cut players, or have some players sit on the bench the entire game. To me, that was a no-win. The only thing worse in my mind would be the job of referee, which is a completely thankless occupation.

Nowadays in basketball, the positions are given numbers and this is a pretty universal standard. The number one is the point guard, in charge of running the plays -- the general on the court. The number two is the shooting guard, responsible for scoring. The number three is the small forward, a hybrid that uses quickness to help the offense while guarding the other team's swingman. The number four is the power forward, someone who posts up on offense, can hit a jumper, and rebound on defense. The number five is the center, typically the biggest player on the team who tries to use size to score and defend. I'm sure if I were playing college ball today, I would be slotted in as a shooting guard. But in the 1960's, this system wasn't really in place. Both guards were responsible for running plays, seeing the floor, and putting other players in positions to be successful. Being a guard helped tremendously as I coached for the first time at the NYCHA clinics. My experiences here allowed me to tell kids where they should be and what they should be doing. As the Varsity coach at Spring Valley High School, I do not utilize the number system the way most other coaches do. We are a small school without much height. I want all my players to get used to handling the ball. My system is more fun for the students but, more importantly, it prepares them for the next level, should they choose to play basketball in college. The money I made from this summer job really came in handy as I returned to school. I would work for the NYCHA again during the summer of 1966. This time, instead of coaching, I mostly went around to the city parks giving motivational speeches.

Even though Claudia and I were married, we were still teenagers so, on some level, I think we were still kind of dating. Every Friday night we would treat ourselves to dinner at a Chinese food restaurant. As the summer was winding down, Claudia suggested we save our date night money and use it to get me a new wardrobe for my sophomore year. I didn't own a suit. Texas Western gave all the players sport jackets to wear. We ended up getting black and gray pants and shirts, and one or two ties. Even though I was headed back South, I think Claudia knew it was time for me to dump the orange and yellow pants. I still wasn't going to win a fashion contest against my teammate David Lattin, but it was an improvement.

Willie Cager had a little amateur mechanic in him. He was good with cars and he came up with a plan for me, him, and Nevil to get back to Texas. He bought a beat up Chevy and we decided to drive it back to El Paso. His plan was for us to drive mostly at night. We would hit less traffic, which would get us better gas mileage and make the trip affordable. We pooled our money for gas and tolls and were on our way. I sat in the back, as usual, with the luggage. However, I had a window seat, so I couldn't have been happier. This was a great trip. I was with two of my best friends in the world and was getting to see the beauty of the United States.

Long car rides give you plenty of time to think. I was on scholarship and knew this season I was moving up to varsity. I figured I was the seventh man, meaning my playing time would come from off the bench. As a sophomore at DeWitt Clinton, when I was told I would be the seventh man, I quit the team. But Etta's birth made me a man, and quitting was no longer an option. I spent most of the ride longing to get back to work on the court. I planned on working harder than ever before to make sure I got playing time. Failure was not an option.

Somewhere in Oklahoma, Cager pulled over to the side of the road. It was about 3 A.M. and I figured it was just another bathroom break. I was wrong. Nevil was asleep and Willie was afraid he was also going to fall asleep -- at the wheel. He told me I had to drive. If I was nervous changing a diaper, think about how I felt driving for the first time in my life on an Oklahoma highway in the middle of the night.

Cager devised what he thought was a foolproof plan. He told me to keep the hood ornament in line with the yellow line on the middle of the road. Even though this would put our car on both sides of the highway, the thinking was that it was so late at night, another car would not be coming the other way. Willie felt the risk of driving down the middle of the highway outweighed the chance of me seeing a cow and driving the car off the road into a ditch. All of a sudden, I longed for "Airplane Mother" to be holding my hand on a flight back to El Paso. We got there safely, although it would not surprise me if Cager had to replace the steering wheel because of how hard I held it during my two hours of driving.

The 1965-1966 Texas Western basketball team consisted of seven black players, four white players, and one Mexican player. Three black players -- myself, David Lattin, and Willie Cager, along with Mexican David Palacio, were all moved from the freshman to varsity squad.

The two starting guards, both black, were Bobby Joe Hill and Orsten Artis. As the third guard, I felt like my skills fell somewhere in the middle of these two men. Bobby Joe was a great penetrator. He was quick off the ball and drove to the basket better than I did. With one more year of experience than me, he was better at running the team – calling the shots while directing traffic on the court. Coach Haskins loved Bobby Joe and allowed him to do things that the rest of us were not allowed to. Bobby was permitted to dribble the ball behind his back and between his legs. Coach Haskins trusted him to do these things without turning the ball over. Bobby Joe was left-handed, and even though everyone knew he was going to drive to the hoop from the left, no one could stop him.

In my mind, Hall of Famer, Oscar "The Big O' Robertson was the best guard to play the game. Orsten Artis was nicknamed "Little O," because he reminded people of Robertson. Ortsten was not the fastest player. He was not the quickest. He was not the biggest. But he was one of the smartest players I have ever seen. He got more out of his athletic ability than anyone around and this man could shoot the ball. I don't know if I ever saw one of his shots hit the backboard or rim. It was always nothing but net. In the way that Bobby Joe had the green light to dribble any way he wanted, Orsten had the green light to shoot jumpers. Because of his amazing basketball I.Q., Orsten was one of our team captains.

Harry "Flo" Flournoy, black, was our other team captain. Harry did the dirty work. He was a defensive specialist and often got the undesirable task of guarding the other team's All-Americans. Harry's contributions extended beyond what happened on the court. Bobby Joe Hill and David Lattin were the star players and the heart of the team. Harry and Orsten, as captains, were the bridge to Coach Haskins. As a senior, Harry had a way of helping get across Coach Haskin's message. Harry and Orsten would never allow things to go bad, on or off the court, and their leadership was instrumental to the success we had during the season.

Nevil Shed, my long time friend, black, was also a key contributor to the team. Nevil was 6'8", so he was often in charge of guarding the other team's big man. Shed was strong defensively and that was certainly going to be rewarded in Coach Haskin's system. Nevil had a good hook shot and contributed offensively as well.

Jerry Armstrong, Louis Baudoin, Dick Myers, and Togo Railey were the four white players on the team. Each of them mostly saw time coming off the bench, and each played an integral part of the success we had, not only in what they contributed during games, but in how they pushed the starters in practice.

Senior Jerry Armstrong was a 6'4" forward. He was nicknamed "The Farmer" because that's what he did during the off-season. The man was a brick house. He also did a lot of the dirty work, physical play necessary in basketball. He would bang around the opposing players and make them uncomfortable. He was a good shooter. He could hit a key jump shot and, overall, he was one hell of a teammate.

Junior Louis "Flip" Baudoin was a 6'7" forward. Like many of our players, he was a lefty. He was a capable shooter and, in practice, he would often take on the role of the opposing player that we were going to face in the game. Coach Haskins always ran an intense practice, and Flip always found a way to break the ice and get the team laughing and joking. He kept us loose when we needed to be loose and that was an amazing skill.

Junior Dick Myers was a cross between a small forward and a big guard. He was a decent athlete and, like me, wasn't very outgoing. Dick was a heady player. His basketball smarts helped him make it as a collegiate athlete.

If you saw junior guard Togo Railey walking around campus, you might have thought he was on the chess team, not the basketball team. At 6'0," the frame of his body was thinner than the frames of his glasses. He had an amazing knowledge of the game. He knew basketball strategy inside and out. Like Flip, he could always make you laugh. And during the stressful times of the 1965-1966 season, those laughs came in handy.

If I wrote this book in the fall of 1965 instead of 2014, my teammates would be surprised that I mentioned their ethnicities during my descriptions. After March 19th, 1966, the differences in our race and culture would come under a microscope. But when the players from New York, Missouri, New Mexico, Indiana, Michigan, Kansas, and Texas came together to start the season, all we saw were other teammates. We didn't see color. We didn't see differences. We saw unity. We were one single team.

Willie Cager and I were roommates during my sophomore year. Bobby Joe and David Lattin were roommates. Harry Flournoy and Orsten Artis were roommates. That means that Nevil Shed had a white roommate and I don't remember who it was. And I think that really says a lot. I don't have a list of stories about a black and white roommate not getting along. It just was not the case. Any argument or disagreement that happened in our dorm of athletes was not caused by race. We all got along and developed a deep personal respect for each other. And we did something else that every college student should make sure to do – we had fun.

A common activity during our down time was to stage massive water fights. We'd fill up buckets of water and go after each other hard. It wasn't a black or white thing. It was a wet thing. And the teams were never black versus white. It was always the small guys versus the big guys. Traveling together on buses and airplanes created a lot of down time for us. We would have marathon card games of Hearts, Spades, and, in particular, Whist. We didn't play poker, because none of us had any money. But because we were athletes, there was a competitive nature in all of us. I'm sure all twelve of us would claim to be the water-fight champion or the best card player there was. Since this is my book, I will claim both of those titles for myself right now.

Roz Worsley is more than just my daughter. She is my advisor, protector, and, in many ways, my best friend. Through the years, I have received offers, some from well-known sportswriters, to write my life story. I never felt the time was right. But when I recently decided to go ahead with this project, I knew that I could not do it without Roz's blessing. I told Roz that an autobiography could be a legacy for my grandchildren. They could see some of the things I've gone through in my life and, in a way I could explain things about myself that I have never opened up about before. Roz wisely pointed out that in many ways, the book would also be for me. She was right. Among many other things, it would give me a chance to pay tribute to my dear friend Bobby Joe Hill.

Of all the relationships I formed by going to Texas Western, none are more important to me than the one I shared with Bobby Joe Hill. He was my brother. With his wavy hair, and good looks, Bobby was a star at El Paso. But unlike some stars, he never got a big head about anything. He was as down-to-earth as they come. He was so laid back, his motto was "Don't sweat it." I can't tell you how many times he said that to me so I'd keep things in perspective. When I'd get nervous, he'd throw a "Don't sweat it" at me, and it always seemed to work.

Bobby Joe was at Texas Western a year before I was and he used his experience to help me. He could see how shy and introverted I was, and he was somewhat the same way. So he made sure that I knew I had someone to talk to and, over the years, we shared our lives with each other. Bobby Joe took me under his wing in regards to basketball as well. Orsten was such a great shooter and he always encouraged me to shoot more. "You can be just as good as Little O." Bobby Joe and I played the same position and yet, he was trying to help me improve. If I got into the game it might mean that he was taken out of the game. He didn't care. He was a team player and, more than that, our friendship was more important than basketball.

Bobby Joe met his future wife Tina while attending Texas Western. Tina was native to El Paso and also attended the school. And since Bobby Joe was my brother, Tina became my sister. The three of us were thick as thieves and spent so much time together. I have some amazing memories of the three of us having fun together. Bobby Joe and Tina married after graduating and stayed in El Paso. Their daughter Michelle became a lawyer and Bobby Joe became an executive at the El Paso Natural Gas Company. Bobby Joe was great for El Paso and El Paso was great for Bobby Joe.

On December 8th, 2002, Bobby Joe had a heart attack. He died. He was only fifty-nine years old. When Tina called to give me the news, I was devastated. It was one of the greatest losses of my entire life. Compounding my loss was the fact that I was not able to attend the services in El Paso because of my financial situation. I had to tell Tina that I would not be there for the funeral. This is still something that haunts me and is one of the biggest regrets of my life. I had spent my life avoiding saying goodbye to the people I love, but this time I needed to say goodbye and couldn't.

This book gives me the opportunity to honor Bobby Joe the way I would have liked to in 2002 after his tragic passing. Instead of saying goodbye, maybe I should use the term farewell. Since I think of him every day, he has never left me. He will be in my heart forever. And Bobby Joe, when we do see each other again someday, do me one favor. Pass me the ball. I promise to shoot.

Chapter 7: The Bear

"When you are where wild bears live, you learn to pay attention to the rhythm of the land and yourself. Bears not only make the habitat rich, they enrich us just by being."
--Linda Jo Hunter, *Lonesome for Bears: A Woman's Journey in the Tracks of the Wilderness*

Don Haskins was nicknamed "The Bear" before I ever set foot on Texas soil. And as the 1965-66 seasons began, he was only thirty-five years old. To me, "The Bear" seems like the nickname of a coach with decades of experience. I envision a coach who has had thousands of players under his charge. But in his short coaching life, Don Haskins roared, groaned, bellowed, growled and instilled enough fear in people that his nickname was well deserved. If I was giving him a nickname, it would have been "The Red Bear," to include how beet red his face would get as he screamed at his players in practice.

Most sport fans, especially football fans, have watched a game played in Denver's Mile High Stadium and heard the announcers talk of the difference in climate. Denver is famous for its thin air, which has a profound effect on athletes. Thin air, especially when your body is not used to it, is more difficult to breathe. What I didn't know when I started my college career was that El Paso had a very similar climate. The thin air made it difficult to breathe and when I would return to school from the Bronx, every inch of my body would notice the difference.

I didn't know what to do about my breathing issues. I felt sluggish, weak, and sometimes I worried that there was something seriously wrong with me. There were times when my nose would just start bleeding, but I didn't want to mention this to anyone. I trained all summer to come back in shape and didn't want Coach Haskins to think otherwise. I finally confided in trainer Ross Moore how I was feeling, and he explained why. He was a great confidant. Ross had a way of communicating to Coach Haskins when a player was injured or needed a break. However, even with Ross's help, our breaks as players were few and far between.

Coach Haskins did not have a soft spot when it came to basketball. "You're not hurt. You're weak between the ears." "You're not tired. If you're not bleeding, you're fine." The most common words out of his mouth were, "Gut up and get after it." Sometimes he would make us have shooting contests to earn water breaks. Most times, water breaks were not part of practice. He was determined to have a team that was tough as nails.

The first week of practice for the 1965-66 season, I ran so much it's amazing that my legs didn't stop working. Coach Haskins would bring us to the field house and have us run stairs for an hour. Up and down the stairs we'd run with no end in sight. At that point, our bodies became almost robotic. If we thought about what we were doing, we'd never have been able to have finished.

Stairs were not the only running we did. He often had us compete in wind sprints against each other. Usually, it was the big guys on the team vs. the little guys. For a guard like me, losing to one of the big guys was deflating. Part of the reason for someone my size to be on the team was my speed, but I have to admit that my dear friend, and team co-captain, Harry Flournoy, would beat me on occasion. The strides of his 6'5" legs were hard for me overcome.

Overall, team practices lasted for around three hours. From a strategic standpoint, most of our practice focused on defense. He instilled in us the importance of defense and I think it saved us in a lot of games that season. If we went into an offensive slump, our strong defensive presence would still enable us to win. Coach Haskins felt that keeping the score down was to our advantage. Sometimes in practice he would make a rule that we had to pass the ball thirty times before we could shoot. There was no shot clock at that time. We were going to win slow, boring games by participating in long, grueling practices. Exercise makes a person hungry, but sometimes the team would be so tired none of us could eat. We'd pull up chairs in the shower and sit for a long time, hoping the water would revive us enough to be able to make it back to the dorms.

Coach Haskins also liked to give players individual attention. I used to call this "getting the extra." "Getting the extra" was not fun and it was not a compliment. It was something that you wanted to avoid but, for most of us, it was inevitable.

Bobby Joe Hill got plenty of extra. When Bobby went home to Detroit in the off-season, he ate whatever he wanted to. He was such a natural that I doubt he even picked up a basketball in the off-season. When he'd return to El Paso, he'd be out of shape. Coach Haskins would call the dining hall and have the kitchen workers put food aside for Bobby Joe because he wouldn't make it there before they closed. Bobby would stay in the gym and get his extra running, extra jumping, and extra harsh words. I was amazed that a coach would treat his best player this way, but Bobby Joe never said a word. Bobby Joe knew that Coach was right.

Nevil Shed got plenty of extra from Coach Haskins. He would stay after practice and be forced to take hook shot after hook shot. Nevil was one of the big guys, so Coach always had him guard a smaller player like me or Bobby Joe. He wanted Nevil to develop his footwork and speed and, in reality, we all became better players by running these drills.

Willie Worsley got plenty, plenty, plenty of extra from Coach Haskins. I was a great shooter in high school, but that only translates to a good shooter in college. Coach Haskins knew being a "good" shooter in college, for someone my size, was not enough. High school basketball is a zone defense game, and college is man-to-man coverage. Man-to-man coverage meant that I would have less open shots. He knew I needed to produce more points with fewer shot attempts.

Coach Haskins put a "shooter rim" inside the regulation rim. This made the basket smaller, and forced me to be more precise with my shot. During my extra, I would sometimes take between three and four hundred shots. When I stood in front of the basket, he wanted my shots to go straight in with nothing but net. When I was to the side of the basket, he wanted my shots to come off the square of the backboard. He knew that I had to develop a high arc on my shot because college was going to have me compete against taller players than I had in high school.

Coach Haskins also knew that someone my size could not afford to be a liability on defense. Coach had me guard Bobby Joe Hill and Orsten Artis in practice as a way of teaching me to defend. Bobby Joe was a penetrator. I learned that I had to force a penetrator to have to pull up and shoot. Orsten was a shooter. I learned that I had to get a shooter out of his comfort zone and make him drive to the basket. As hard as I tried, Bobby ultimately ran around me and Orsten shot over me. If they kept a stat about chasing people in practice, I would have definitely led our team.

As a varsity basketball coach, I hate watching game film. I leave that job to my assistant coach, Tony. I do my scouting during the first quarter of a game. But Coach Haskins loved to show game film. Nowadays, most colleges have video coordinators who probably make a lot of money. Back then, we were sat down in a small room watching black and white film on rickety old film projectors. I have to admit there were times that I found myself drifting off to sleep from the boredom. Coach Haskins had more than just X's and O's on his mind when he showed us game film. If we ever played against a bad team, he would never show us the film. If we played against a good team, he would only show us the parts he wanted to. Usually, those were the parts where we made mistakes. If part of the film was about to show us going on a run, he would have Moe Iba flip on the lights and he'd start talking to us. He was a master psychologist. He knew how to work our minds and our emotions.

One of the hardest things to do as a coach is to coach talent. That might seem like an odd statement, but it is true. High expectations for a team can sometimes be the kiss of death. Some talented athletes get too cocky or don't work hard enough in practice. Good athletes know they can turn it on like a faucet, but sometimes they turn it on too late. In addition to that, opponents always give their best efforts against a talented team. If we won a game by ten points, Coach Haskins would tell us after the game we should have won by fifty. He never wanted us to get complacent.

I'm sure there were times during my college career that I hated Coach Haskins for constantly chewing me and my teammates out. There were times that playing for that man was hell on earth. However, I realize that he instilled in me life lessons that have made me a better person to this day. And for that, I have a great love and respect for Coach. Deep down, he was a loving and caring person.

Coach Haskins taught me the benefit of staying even-keeled. When you are riding high, it is a long way to fall. When you are down, it feels like a long way to the top. You are never as good or as bad as people say you are. When I was high, he would tell me about things I could have done better. When he could tell I was feeling low, he would point out what an amazing thing I was doing for my family back in New York. When I would glare at Coach Haskins in practice the way I would at Moe Iba during my freshman season, Coach would make me stop contorting my face. It wasn't because he cared one bit if I was mad at him, but he never wanted my opponent in a game to have an insight into my emotions. He taught me to act the same way after a good or bad play. Eventually, when I got mad at him, my facial contortions would become a smile.

Coach Haskins taught me the importance of a strong work ethic. Many people plateau at something after they are good at it. It's hard to become great. Greatness is something that has to be earned, and once it is you have to work twice as hard to maintain it.

In 1986, there was a reunion in El Paso to celebrate the team that played in the March 19th, 1966 N.C.A.A Championship Game. In addition to players, the coaches, assistant coaches, and trainers were all invited. It was one of the most touching ceremonies of my life

A man named Joe Gomez deserves much of the credit for making this event happen. Joe was an El Paso lifelong resident and businessman. Bobby Joe Hill remained there after his college days, and he and Joe became close friends. Joe Gomez did not want the community to forget about our team. To him, it was an important part of the fabric of the city. Joe petitioned local businesses for support and then presented the school with his plan to have the old Texas Western team get together. Through Joe's efforts, the entire team and their families were on hand to be honored during halftime of a home game.

Each person associated with the team was given a beautiful, expensive ring -- possibly designed by Joe. Along with the name Willie Worsley, my number 24 was engraved on the side of my ring. It was so personal and it made me realize that even though we were out of sight, we were not completely out of the minds of the El Paso faithful. Everyone there treated the players and their wives like kings and queens. Along with my Naismith Memorial Hall of Fame Ring that I received in 2007, this ring is the most important treasure from my playing career. This is why I have given both of these rings to the greatest treasure of my life, Roz.

When I landed in El Paso as a teenager, I could not believe that I was immediately interviewed by the local media. In 1986, I was surprised all over again that there was such interest in us. Reporters asked me a ton of questions and it almost felt like I'd never left. They hadn't forgotten about "Wee" Willie Worsley, which is what I was always called by the El Paso press. Many of the questions were about Coach Haskins, and through talking to some of the players and, in particular, the public relations director Ed Mullins, I came to realize something that I had never fully known the extent of before.

From 1966-1986, and possibly after that as well, Coach Haskins had received a constant barrage of death threats. In the movie *A Miracle on 34th Street*, the Santa character is saved at the end of the movie by duffle bags full of letters of love and hope from little kids. Suddenly, I pictured Coach Haskins with duffle bags full of hate letters somewhere in the back of the pickup truck he would always drive around town: hate letters that were sent to him by white people: hate letters that were sent to him by black people. And yet, he never told me directly about any of this. I don't think he talked about it in great detail with his players, even through the passage of time. By the time of the reunion, I was older than Coach Haskins had been when he had coached me. It pained me to think that he had been carrying around all of that hate by himself for so long.

Bears do more than roar, groan, bellow and growl. Bears protect their cubs. During the 1965-66 season, Coach Haskins did a lot to protect his team. I think sometimes being a coach is a life-long job.

On December 4th, 1965, we played our first game of the season. Bobby Joe Hill, Orsten Artis, Harry Flournoy, Nevil Shed, and David Lattin were the starters. I saw a lot of action in the game and we won big. It was my first varsity game and, in addition to the excitement of winning, I enjoyed the fact that the game was easier than participating in any of Coach Haskins' practices. I figured now that I hit the big time, a gourmet meal would be awaiting the team for our post game dinner. What would they have for us – a nice juicy steak with all the trimmings? I was unpleasantly surprised when I was given a brown paper bag with a bologna and cheese sandwich and an apple. If you had told me then, while I chewed on my rubbery bologna, dreaming of my imaginary steak, that the game I just played would start a string of events that would result in death threats, I don't think I could have ever believed you.

Chapter 8: The Season

"A small body of determined spirits fired by an unquenchable faith in their mission can alter the course of history." –Mahatma Ghandi

    I think the most stress I ever felt as a collegiate player happened about ten minutes before our first game of the 1965-1966 season. We were facing New Mexico State and when Coach Haskins gave me my first assignment, a fear and dread entered my being. What if I make a mistake? What if I embarrass myself? Why am I being asked to do something that I've never done before? "Little Man," Coach Haskins said, while shoving a basketball into my gut, "At this level in college, players are introduced in size order from shortest to tallest. You need to jump through the circular paper banner held by the cheerleaders and lead us onto the court." I once played in front of a sold out Madison Square Garden, but this task made me much more nervous than that did. I think I pictured myself falling after breaking through the paper, or possibly running to the wrong bench. I felt like some embarrassing mishap awaited me and, just like I had many other times in my life, I wished I was taller. Luckily, none of those things happened.
    Waiting around for the New Mexico State game to start, which we won 89-38, I got my first exposure to Coach Haskins' pre-game rituals, and just like everything else Coach Haskins did, it was intense and extreme. Out of nowhere, he yelled, "Lights Out!" and someone ran and flipped off the light switch. He told us that he wanted us to sit in the dark for a half hour and think about tonight's game. I didn't know what to do. At first, I didn't think there was any way he could be serious, but then I remembered that everything he did was serious. So I just sat there, and I don't think I really thought about the game at all. I may have a little bit, but a half hour in silence feels like an eternity. A half-hour television show might feel like it flies by, but this time in the dark crawled by second by second. My mind drifted away and I thought of Etta, and Claudia, and my mother. I thought about this and that until finally, Coach Haskins screamed for the lights to be put back on. When they came on, I looked around to see what would happen next. Harry and Orsten were the team captains, so I followed their leads. They jumped into a line, almost like we were in the military and Coach Haskins was our drill sergeant. He walked up and down and basically told us that we were not ready. He knew we were cocky about our abilities, and I think that was his biggest worry about our team. He did not want overconfidence to bring about our downfall. Before he finished his inspection up and down the line, he would shake every player's hand. If your hand wasn't sweaty, he would yell

at you. He felt that if your hand wasn't sweaty, you weren't ready. As the season went on, my hand would never sweat because I wasn't nervous. I was excited to play each game, but not nervous enough to sweat. Each time I presented Coach my dry hand, he gave me plenty of pre-game "extra." Finally, I devised a plan to get out of being chewed out before each game. Whenever I'd enter a locker room for a road game, I would scope out where the nearest water fountain was. When the announcement for "Lights Out" was made, I would tip-toe over to the fountain and put water on my hand. It worked, and Coach Haskins was happy that I was finally mentally preparing the right way.

By the time we played Fresno State, on December 17th, 1965, we were 4-0. We defeated New Mexico, East Texas State, Texas Pan American, and Weber State. As a team, we were feeling good about ourselves and that was probably the last thing in the world Coach Haskins wanted. Fresno State had speed. Speed was our biggest strength, but they were fast as well. They were good ball handlers and did a good job of withstanding our defensive pressure. We won the game 75-73, but afterwards, Coach Haskins really let us have it. He chewed us out big time. You may assume that a coach would be happy as long as the team won, but this was not the case with Coach Haskins. "Why would we let a team we should dominate almost beat us? Why would we risk throwing away our season on a team we should manhandle?" Coach Haskins looked at the Fresno State game as a bad omen for our season. Luckily for us, on December 18th, we played Fresno State again. Nowadays in college, playing back-to-back games like this probably wouldn't happen. But back then, to save on travel costs, games were sometimes scheduled in this manner. We won the second Fresno State game 83-65. I'm sure we still got chewed out because we always did. However, I think the score differential was a sign that all the players got the message. There are no guaranteed wins in college sports. There are no guaranteed wins in any sports; you get as many points as you can, period.

The scheduling of college basketball games is an intricate process. Every team within a league will play all other league teams twice a season. This leaves several open dates on a season schedule that need to be filled in by teams outside of the league. Small and middle-sized schools love to play the big time programs, because it translates into money. High profile teams fill the arena, and there is a split of the money taken in at the gate. High profile teams might look at smaller programs as an easy win and agree to take the game. Back then, it was also a way for big schools to play in smaller towns and cities and, in a roundabout way, to recruit new players. If a school was popular, like Duke or Kentucky, they had an easier time convincing a top recruit to come play at their school.

On December 30th, 1965, we were scheduled to play Iowa State. They were the fourth ranked team in the nation and, as I look back, I'm almost a little surprised they agreed to play us at Memorial Gym in El Paso;

sometimes big programs are afraid to play the smaller schools in a road game. They figure the small school might get some "home cooking," which is what I call the referees' inclination to give the home team the best of the calls. I'm not sure how Coach Haskins got them to agree to come. My guess is that the game was set up years in advance and that Iowa State did not follow our freshman team. If they had scouted us, they would have seen the quality of our players. David Lattin, a future first round pick in the N.B.A., would have played varsity his freshman year if the N.C.A.A. rules allowed it.

Coach Haskins hyped up Iowa to his players. He wanted us to recognize the magnitude of this game. Playing a good game against a ranked team would be a positive for our school's program. A victory over the #4 ranked Iowa would be a benchmark win. That week in practice we worked harder than ever and, as I've already described our practices, you know that is saying something. He wanted us guarding their players the second they got off the bus. If he could have had us set pick and rolls as Iowa walked to the locker room to change into their uniforms, he would have. I think he really wanted us to establish ourselves within the first ten minutes of the game. If we played our game, we were good enough to beat them. If they saw that we were good enough to beat them, the pressure would shift to them as the favored team. Coach Haskins, the master psychologist, did a great job of mentally preparing us for our biggest challenge to date. When the game was eight minutes old, even though the score was close, I knew we were going to win. They could not handle our man-to-man defense. We were too fast and too balanced. We took them out of their comfort zones. Their shooters were forced to penetrate. Their penetrators were forced to shoot low percentage shots. I even think the thin air of El Paso played to our advantage. As the game progressed, and they became increasingly tired, our amazing team conditioning became a big factor.

We were winning at halftime and, in a weird way, I almost think Coach Haskins would have preferred it if we were down by a point or two. He did not want us to get complacent. He did not want us to mentally put this game in the win column until the final buzzer sounded and we were ahead. He gave a rousing halftime speech and demanded that we start the second half by making a statement. Our statement was that our team refused to lose this game. We won the game 86-68, and we were now 10-0 on the season.

At the time, the game against Iowa State was the most important of my collegiate career. It showed that Texas Western could play with the big boys and that our program was officially big time. When we got back to the dorm to celebrate, the bag lunch of a peanut butter and jelly sandwich and an apple just wasn't going to cut it. Bobby Joe and I slipped out for some delicious El Paso foot-long chili dogs. Athletes are creatures of habit and superstition and to this day, a foot-long chili dog is still my after game treat following an important victory.

Coach Haskins was thrilled about our win versus Iowa State, but at the same time he was worried -- he was always worried. That's one of the things that made him great. If the Iowa win made us more confident than we already were as a team, there was a good chance that we would take an opponent lightly somewhere along the way and ruin our season. The speech at practice following the Iowa win was almost like a sermon. He hammered home the point that a win against a big team followed by a loss to a lesser team would be one step forward and two steps back. We had to maintain our hunger.

I think the schedule gods gave us the perfect next opponent following the Iowa game. It was certainly the perfect opponent for Coach Haskins to work his psychological magic on the players. And I was an integral part of his master plan.

On January 3rd, 1966, we played Tulsa. Tulsa's best player was a 6'2" guard named Elgin Webb. Elgin and I had a history. He was the star player for Boys High School in Brooklyn when I was playing for Dewitt Clinton. We were our team's best players when the high school championship was played in Madison Square Garden in 1963. And even though my team came away with the victory, there was always a part of me that felt that a majority of people looked at him as a better player. We were both all-city, but because his style was basic and mine was fancy, I think people expected that he could jump right into collegiate basketball easier than I could. If you've read this book up to this point, you know that "Iron Head" does not take being disrespected lightly.

Coach Haskins knew about our history. Throughout the practice days leading up to the game, he did not get on my case. He did not give me any of the "extra." He let me be, but he also made sure that the rest of my teammates knew what this game meant for me to win. Coach told me that I was getting the start and that I would guard Elgin man-to-man. I think they would have had to restrain me if I was told someone else was given that assignment. For me, this game was personal.

This game really highlights the importance of the team concept. My teammates, who were also my dear friends, made me the main focus of the game. I got more passes than usual. I felt like more plays were run through me. My teammates liked and respected me and they rallied around me as a show of support. By getting the team to rally around me, Coach Haskins prevented us from having a let-down game following the huge win versus Iowa. I had one of my best games of the season and we won 63-54.

My rivalry versus Elgin Webb was not really personal; it was professional. I liked him as a person. We were a lot alike: quiet in nature, outwardly modest, etc. We just represented a challenge to each other and we probably pushed each other to get better. After the game, I treated Elgin to some delicious El Paso chili dogs. As much as we were rivals, we were also just two New York City kids living out a dream thousands of miles away from home.

The game versus Tulsa was important for more than the pride I felt in how my team supported me. It was the last game of the season in which we were not ranked nationally. Before we played Seattle on January 6, 1966, we were ranked #9 in the country. And when we beat Seattle that night 76-64, we moved up to #6.

About a month after the Seattle game, we were still ranked #6 and we were still undefeated -- having beaten Arizona State twice, West Texas State, and New Mexico. We also hit a very tough stretch of our schedule. On February 4th, 1966, we played Colorado State in Fort Collins, Colorado. This game was a battle. Colorado had a huge guard named Lonnie Wright; Lonnie was 6'2" and two hundred and thirty pounds of pure muscle. We all took turns trying to guard him and we all took turns failing. He gave Bobby Joe hell. Then he gave Orsten hell. Then he gave me hell. It was the first time in my life I felt overmatched physically. My best defense didn't seem to bother him at all. He could ball handle perfectly, was a great shooter, and was as fast as I was. My speed was always an advantage I had over an opponent, but it was canceled out by Lonnie's abilities. I had to use strategy to guard him. I made him turn his back to the basket he was going to shoot at. I wanted him to worry about me stealing the ball. If he had this worry in the back of his mind, I hoped it would make him think twice about penetrating. I tried to make him run into the help my bigger teammates gave me by collapsing down on him. It was a back and forth game but somehow we won, 68-66. Sometimes in sports, it is better to be lucky than good and I always felt we were lucky to win that game. Had we lost, who knows how the rest of the season would have played out?

On February 12th, 1966 we had another battle on our hands. We played New Mexico State at the Johnson Gymnasium in Albuquerque. The arena was nicknamed "the pit," partly because it was sunk down in the earth like the basement of a house, and partly because of the hostile environment it provided. The fans showed up dressed alike in a sea of red shirts and screamed and cheered from start to finish. Even with all the momentum we had built up during the season, I felt during this game that our backs were up against the wall.

New Mexico was a well coached team. Not only that, but they were much bigger than we were. Their guards used strength to neutralize our speed. Their forwards, for the most part, manhandled our forwards. New Mexico also had something else that we needed to deal with -- Mel Daniels.

About a year after our game with New Mexico, Mel Daniels was drafted in the first round of the N.B.A. draft. He was also drafted by the A.B.A. and won two championships with the Indiana Pacers. He became one of the greatest players in A.B.A. history, and here we were trying to guard a man who was ready for the pros. Mel was from Detroit, and he and Bobby Joe were friends, and basketball rivals, in high school. In the same way, the worst way, that I wanted to win my game versus Elgin Webb, Bobby wanted to beat Mel Daniels.

New Mexico was beating us by sixteen points by the time the buzzer sounded for halftime. I felt like our undefeated season was surely coming to an end. Not only that, but we risked losing our national ranking. We entered the game ranked #4, but a loss here would have taken that away from us. We just did not have an answer for Mel Daniels.

Bobby Joe Hill was always the strong silent type. He led more by example than with words. He was not the "rah rah" type in the locker room, but losing by sixteen points to his friend and rival Mel was more than he could take. Bobby Joe stepped forward. He was as emotional as I had ever seen him before in my life. He told us that he refused to lose this game and that we had all better plan on entering the second half with the same attitude. Bobby Joe was David Lattin's best friend on the team. David, our center, had the undesirable assignment of guarding Mel. Bobby Joe challenged David. He challenged David to go out and have the best game of his life.

The challenge worked. David played the second half like a man possessed. So did Bobby Joe. I don't know if either of them missed a shot. Little by little, the sixteen point lead became smaller and smaller. Ultimately, we won the game 67-64 in overtime and kept our undefeated season intact. We were now 18-0 and would still be ranked #4 as we entered our next game against Arizona. Bobby Joe's halftime speech may have saved our season.

From there, we beat Arizona State, Texas, West Texas State, Colorado, and New Mexico. The last game of our regular season took place on March 5th, 1966. It was a road game versus Seattle. Our record was 23-0. Before Coach demanded we shut off the lights and meditate for a half hour, he talked to the team. He told us that if we won this game, we would be the #1 ranked team in the country. We were currently ranked #2. We had never spent a day of the season in the #1 spot and, without doing research, I feel safe in assuming that Texas Western had never been ranked #1 at anything up to that point -- besides maybe teaching people how to work in a coal mine. We had a chance at making history. Unfortunately, we missed that chance.

I don't know if it was exactly one thing that went wrong. Maybe Coach Haskins had a rare misstep by telling us the magnitude of the game. Maybe we were over confident from all the big games we won during the year. Maybe we were over confident because two months earlier we beat Seattle 76-64. Whatever the reason, we did not play our game. I don't want to take anything away from Seattle, but this had to be our worst game of the season. We didn't play like a team. We played more "I" and less "we." Some players pressed, while other players seemed lazy for the first time all season. And with as bad as we played, we still almost won. The final score was 74-72. Three points were all that separated us from an undefeated season, a rarity in college basketball. I can't imagine how many times Coach Haskins warned us not to let a team stick around in a game. I can't imagine how many times he warned us about being over confident. His worries became a reality -- the last game of the season!

We did not fly home to El Paso that night. And just like young people will sometimes do, to make matters worse, we left our motel after curfew and snuck off into the dark, rainy Seattle night. I'm not sure if we were looking for fun or looking for trouble. We were probably just looking for anything that would help us temporarily forget the pain of our first loss of the season.

When we finally returned to our motel, in the middle of the night, our room doors were all wide open. Coach Haskins had caught us and he wanted us to know that he did before we went to sleep. I mentioned that if I could have picked his nickname, it would have been the "Red Bear" to signify the color of his face when he got mad. I have a feeling his face was the color of a fire truck when he saw we had the nerve to leave that night. The next morning, he did not let us sleep in. He ran us to death, and when he thought some of us might literally drop dead in front of him, he ran us to death again. He didn't yell and, by not yelling, it actually made us all more nervous than usual. I think it was the only time in my life I was actually frightened of what he might do to me. When we boarded the plane, he still did not let us sleep. He had Moe Iba and Ross Moore go up and down the aisles and keep us awake. If we wanted to stay up having so much fun while avoiding sleep, he was going to accommodate us.

Our next game was on March 6th. It was a road game. Actually, it was a neutral site game. We flew into Wichita, Kansas to play Oklahoma City. It was the first game of the N.C.A.A. tournament. Our loss to Seattle didn't keep us out of the playoffs. In fact, in retrospect, I think the loss to Seattle might have been the best thing to happen to us. It brought us back down to earth. It gave us the bitter taste of defeat, and none of us wanted to know that feeling again. It taught us the truth in Coach Haskins' words about being over -- confident. I think the loss helped provide us with the hunger we needed as we entered the post season.

So, a very sleepy Texas Western squad faced off against Oklahoma City in the first game of the tournament. Oklahoma was one of the top scoring teams in the nation. They liked to use a fast break offense to get up the court and score points. Our strong defense didn't allow that to happen. We made them play a half court offense, and this brought down the usual number of points they were accustomed to scoring. Once we did this, we took over. We turned our defense into offense and won the game 89-74. The way a team reacts to a loss, in particular a first loss of the season, is very important. The fact that we came back out and took control was a good sign moving forward.

Our next game took place on March 11th, 1966. As players, I think we lucked out that they gave us a couple of days off. The games were shown on weekends for better television ratings, and Coach finally let us all get some sleep. I guess our punishment for the Seattle sneak out was finally over.

Cincinnati was one of the best teams we played all season. They were like us in the sense that they prided themselves on strong defensive play. However, like a lot of teams, they were bigger than we were. They had a seven foot center who looked like a skyscraper and we were over-matched physically. We just never gave up. The game was very nip and tuck. They would go on a scoring run and then we'd come back and go on a scoring run. The buzzer sounded at the end of overtime; I looked up at the scoreboard and saw that we won 78-76. I couldn't believe it. There were times during the game that I thought we might lose by fifty points, but we gutted it out as a unit. A basketball game that close, decided in overtime, really proves the cliché about sports being a game of inches. One shot here, one foul here, one turnover there, was all it took for one team to move on and the other team to go home for good. I felt lucky that we were the ones that were getting to stick around.

On April 9th, 1982, Jo Jo White had his number retired by the Boston Celtics, the most successful franchise in N.B.A history. In the 1970's, he won two world championships with the team and in 1976 he was even the finals M.V.P. To many basketball experts, he is the best player not inducted into the Naismith Memorial Basketball Hall of Fame. I'm not sure why he isn't. I hope this description gives you an idea of how good a player Jo Jo White was, because he is what stood in our way on March 12, 1966. If we won the game against Jo Jo and his powerful Kansas team, we'd make it to the N.C.A.A final four. If we lost, it would be the final game of our season.

Jo Jo was not the only star on Kansas. They had another All-American in Walt Wesley. Coach Haskins tried to bill this as our All-Americans versus theirs. He knew that we needed our two best players, Bobby Joe Hill and David Lattin, to match the performances of their two best players if we had any chance to win. This was no easy task.

David and Nevil did a good job containing Walt Wesley, but I had a tough time with Jo Jo. At 6'4", he had a good size advantage over me. Jo Jo knew how good he was. He had a star quality swagger as he moved up and down the court. He was smooth as silk and his shot was the "truth." He was a player that was hyped by the media and he lived up to the hype that game. It did not surprise me when he was eventually selected in the first round of the N.B.A draft. He was the best guard on the floor that night and it seemed that every shot he took went in. Luckily, my teammates were scoring too and the game became like a boxing match with two great heavyweights standing toe-to-toe exchanging fierce body shots.

The winner was decided in the second overtime. It was a double dose of sudden death with the entire season on the line for two great teams. We were winning 81-80 but Kansas had the ball. A Jayhawk kicked the ball out to Jo Jo White in the corner. How did we let him get his hands on the ball?

Everyone in the arena knew they were going to him, and we didn't stop it. If he didn't get his hands on the ball, he couldn't shoot and beat us. He got the shot off, and if you are a basketball fan you know that sometimes you can tell a shot is going in the second it leaves a player's hand. I knew it was going in the second Jo Jo let it fly. I was right. The ball went in and the scoreboard read 82-81, Kansas.

I sat on the bench staring at the floor, using my hands to hold up my head. My body felt like complete jelly. We just lost the game. We just lost our chance to continue on in the N.C.A.A. playoffs and, for me, I just lost a chance to play on the East Coast. If we had won the game, we would next fly to Maryland for the final four. I had fantasies of my East Coast family and friends from the Bronx coming south to see me play. My dream was dead. Or was it?

All of a sudden, I noticed my teammates jumping up and down in utter and sheer joy. What the hell is going on? The referee disallowed Jo Jo White's shot. He said that Jo Jo had stepped on the out of bounds line while shooting, so the basket did not count. I could not believe it. The scoreboard was changed to read Texas Western 81, Kansas 80. It was almost like waking up from a nightmare. Sometimes, when you wake up from a nightmare you need time to calm yourself down and convince yourself that it was all a dream. That's what happened to me. Even seeing all my teammates jumping around didn't do it for me. It really took some time for the enormity of the call to sink in. And to that end, I have to say how impressed I am that the referee made the call – a call that I know in my heart was the correct call. Even though it was a neutral site game, the crowd was certainly rooting for Kansas. That was usually the case for all of our neutral site games and we certainly had a tough time on the road, but he had the guts to do what he knew was right. I know from a life in basketball that that is not always easy to do. In the blink of an eye we were off to the Cole Field House in College Park, Maryland, to participate in the final four.

On Friday afternoon, March 18th, 1966, Kentucky played Duke in the first matchup of the N.C.A.A final four. For most fans and people in the media, this was the actual championship game. Most people figured whoever came out of this contest would steamroll either Texas Western or our final four opponent, Utah. Kentucky beat Duke and so we knew who we would play if we could somehow get past Utah. And I think that for the first time before a game, we got emotional as a team. We felt disrespected and, from a basketball standpoint, we wanted a chance to go out and prove to the world how good we were. However, we knew we had to get past Utah first. We couldn't come this far and fail.

Utah had an excellent player in Jerry Chambers. His arms were as long as two days and he could shoot with the best of them. Many of us took turns guarding him, but with little success. That's when Coach Haskins knew he had to try something, anything, if we were going to pull this game out. Coach decided to put in Jerry Armstrong to guard Chambers. Jerry Armstrong had been successfully coming in off the bench all season, and he picked the right time to have one of his best games. Even though Chambers probably scored close to thirty points, when Jerry Armstrong came in Chambers started to slow down. Jerry Armstrong, without a doubt, won that game for us and it highlights how much of a team effort it took to make it to the championship versus Kentucky. The final score was 85-78 us.

All of us, even Coach Haskins, were elated following the win versus Utah. We were scheduled to play Kentucky the following day to decide the National Champion. And here is where I think Coach Haskins made one of his best coaching moves ever. He made a deal with us. He told us that if we promised to stay in our rooms, he wouldn't enforce a curfew. It was genius. We were so amped up from the win that none of us would have been able to sleep. By letting us be together, it gave us the opportunity to blow off steam. We trash talked, joked about this and that, and got to go back to being kids for just a little while.

We played the card game Whist, like we had on the planes and buses around the country, for countless hours, and this helped a lot. It took our minds off of the obvious – we were one win away from winning a National Championship and becoming a part of history by getting our names in the record book. What none of us realized was that whether we won or lost the game, when the referee threw the jump ball in the air to start the game versus Kentucky, history would already be made!

Chapter 9: The Ladder

"In each age men of genius undertake the ascent. From below, the world follows them with their eyes. These men go up the mountain, enter the clouds, disappear, reappear. People watch them, mark them. They walk by the side of precipices. They daringly pursue their road. See the aloft, see them in the distance; they are but black specks. On they go. The Road is uneven, its difficulties constant. At each step a wall, at each step a trap. As they rise the cold increases. They must make their ladder, cut the ice and walk on it, hewing the steps in haste. A storm is raging. Nevertheless they go forward in their madness. The air becomes difficult to breath. The abyss yawns below them. Some fall. Others stop and retrace their steps; there is a sad weariness. The bold ones continue. They are eyed by the eagles; the lightning plays about them: the hurricane is furious. No matter, they persevere."
-Victor Hugo

When we played our first game of the season, versus Eastern New Mexico State on December 4th, 1965, Coach Haskins began his normal pregame routine. Before demanding that the lights be shut, he would write the names of the starters on the blackboard. On that first night, he wrote the names, Bobby Joe, Orsten, David, Harry, and Willie. Willie Cager started at forward. And with a piece of chalk, Coach Haskins broke an unwritten rule of college basketball. It was unwritten because if the rule was written, it would have been illegal. Coach Haskins was sending five black men out to start an N.C.A.A basketball game. And in the 1960's, this simply was not done.

Don Haskins did not try to become a civil rights trailblazer. He did not try to become a sports trailblazer or any other kind of trailblazer. However, when the role of trailblazer was thrust upon him he never avoided it either. Coach Haskins played for a Hall of Famer in Henry Iba, and he wanted to do anything possible to be the best coach he could. If he was going to amass wins and championships like Moe Iba's father Henry had done, he was going to need to coach some good teams. So when Coach Haskins put together his first starting lineup of the season, he did it because he felt that those players were the best combination for a winning formula. If a white player would have made us a better team, he would have played that person in a heartbeat. He treated us all the same ---- badly -- and I say that with one hundred percent love and respect in my heart. He didn't see us as black or white. He saw us as players. He didn't see us as two separate groups. He saw us as one united team. And for that decision, he received a lifetime of hate mail and death threats.

Racism and hatred was as much a part of our 1965-1966 season as dribbling, passing, and shooting. There were some buildings where we'd play without much of an obvious issue. There were other times we'd walk in a building and feel the wrath immediately. I'd hear people yell "nigger" at us with such venom, and to this day I still find it so troubling to hear anyone, of any race, use this horrible slur. There were times when we'd have things thrown at us from the stand, usually the remnants of what people picked up at the food counters in the arena hallways. The New York City instincts in me, Willie Cager, and Nevil Shed were to not take disrespect from anyone. In New York City, that was survival. But what were we to do? Coach Haskins refused to let us take the bait. He would point out the obvious, that we could not take on thousands of people all by ourselves. The entire team was affected by the physical and verbal abuse we took. Our white teammates were our brothers, and they felt just as helpless as we did. In addition to getting mentally prepared to face our opponents on the court, we had to have a game plan on how to deal with many of the hate filled crowds we faced on the road.

There were times when we felt that it was possible that racism was influencing some of the calls referees were making. David Lattin must have fouled out in close to a dozen games that season. He was a physical player, but often star collegiate players are given the benefit of the doubt when it comes to fouls and keeping them in the game. But that never seemed to work for David. And at the same time, we played some games where little or no fouls were called against the opposing team. In a real basketball game, that is basically impossible. Even though Jo Jo White was black, Kansas did have white starters and therefore they were favored by the crowd over us. And that is why I was so complimentary of the referee for having the integrity to make the right call and say that Jo Jo stepped out of bounds. It would have been very easy for him to look the other way. Many people would have been happy to have the one team starting five black players eliminated from the tournament. Coach Haskins was receiving letters from people who wanted him eliminated from the planet.

Texas Western had "The Bear," and the Kentucky Wildcats had "The Baron." Adolf Rupp, Kentucky's coach, was probably one of the most famous men in the Bluegrass state by the time our teams collided in March of 1966. He was, and is, one of the most famous basketball coaches of all time. When his career was over, he had won over 800 games and four national championships. He started coaching in 1930, the same year Don Haskins was born. But besides colorful nicknames and reputations for brutal practices, I think a lot of basketball historians looked at them as two very different men.

There were rumors for years that Adolf Rupp was prejudiced against black collegiate players. The entire Kentucky team we played that night was white, and there had been persistent talk that he had refused for decades to coach a black player. I am paraphrasing, but as players we heard he said something to the effect of "he was not going to lose to five black boys." Supposedly that was said around the time of a contentious press conference between Coach Haskins and Rupp, where Rupp seemed arrogant about his team's chances and Coach Haskins seemed to have to justify our being there. If there was a Guinness Book World Record for the most times a person has been asked a question about someone they never met, my teammates and I probably hold it. From 1966 until the present, I have been asked countless times my opinion on whether or not Adolf Rupp was a racist. And every time I have been asked, I choose my words with care. I am a "tell it like it is person," but I never wanted to have my words twisted or used as a sound bite for a sportscaster or journalist. Since I am writing my autobiography, I will probably put down here as much as I've ever said on the matter. It is possible people will not be satisfied with my answer to the question of whether Rupp was a racist or not.

    The truth of the matter is I have no idea what was in that man's heart. The only time we were in the same room, if you can call it a room, was in the Cole Field House the night of March 19th, 1966. People who claim that Rupp refused to coach black players point to the decades in which he had an all-white team. There was talk of several top black recruits going to Kentucky to walk around campus, but none, until the very end of his career, ever joined the team. Again I am paraphrasing, but supposedly Rupp mentioned that a black player in the South would be treated so poorly that he didn't want to be responsible for the racism of the crowds his team would play in front of. Rupp detractors called on him and his incredible influence in college sports to help the civil rights movement, while others questioned why he was being singled out as a racist when plenty of other coaches were not integrating their teams. Being falsely accused of something is one of the most terrible things that can happen to a person. If Adolf Rupp's intentions were misunderstood, I have pity for the man. If people were correct in characterizing his actions as racist, then I can't help but appreciate the irony. It's possible that a racist attitude actually brought attention to, and helped advance, the civil rights movement not only in sports, but in the entire 1960's America.

    It was an hour before the game and Coach Haskins took out a piece of chalk and lumbered towards the blackboard. As usual, he wrote the starting lineup for the game. He put up the names Bobby Joe, Orsten, David, Harry, and Willie. I immediately went over to encourage my roommate Willie Cager to have the game of his life. Coach Haskins stopped me. "No, I mean you little one." Coach Haskins had decided to start me, a third guard, in the biggest game of our lives. I didn't say a word. I did not ask him why because I was trained not to ask him why. I hadn't questioned him before the previous twenty-eight games and this wasn't a good time to start.

    When Coach Haskins wrote the lineup on the board, history was made. We would be the first all-black starting lineup in an N.C.A.A. Championship game. To be one of those starting five is a point of pride with me that has lasted a lifetime. And at the same time, it's important to realize that if I didn't start, we still would have been the first all-black starting lineup. Willie Cager would have started. Or maybe it would have been Nevil Shed. We had five black starters the entire season. This was our norm. Eventually, when we went to play the game, this historic twist was not in our minds. Coach Haskins didn't start us to prove a point to the world about race. He started us because he wanted to win a basketball game. And when we took the floor, we did not try our best to influence the civil rights movement or disprove the opinions of racists. We wanted to be national champions.

When Coach called for the lights to be shut so we could think about the game for a half hour in silence, for the first time all season I felt like I had plenty to think about. I thought about the day during my senior year of high school when we got our first television. It was a fourteen inch black and white set, and my mother and I saved up for a long time to buy it. And now, because we bought that television, my mother would be able to see me play basketball for the first time in her life. This night, she finally let herself miss a day of work. Since Claudia was able to make it from the Bronx to Maryland, my mother had babysitting duty. My beautiful Etta would be on her lap, watching her daddy and even though she was so young, my heart knows she was cheering for me more than anyone else. And because there was such a small window of my life where I owned a television, I realized that I had never seen an N.C.A.A Championship game before. This night would be the first time I would see one, and I was in the starting lineup.

From the moment I ran out onto the floor for pre-game introductions by the arena P.A. announcer, I got that vibe that we were once again in a hostile environment. As I looked past all the cameras into the audience, there was a sea of white faces staring down at us. There were very few black spectators. There were also very few black reporters, cheerleaders, or any other person of color besides our team. This didn't negatively affect me. It motivated me just the way I always feel motivated when I feel I am up against the odds. When our team broke out of the huddle and ran back to the bench, none of us had to say a word. We knew what was at stake.

Coach Haskins had a plan to win the game. He predicted, correctly, that Kentucky was going to play a zone defense against us. There was a stereotype back then that black players were not good shooters. Since I wasn't invited into Kentucky's pre-game meeting, I don't know if that was the reason for their strategy. Coach Haskins figured they would try to keep the ball away from our big man David Lattin and force us to shoot from the outside. Since I was a better long range shooter than Nevil, my skills may be useful against a zone. By putting a third guard on the floor, me, we were giving something away in size. I was assigned to guard Kentucky forward Tommy Kron. He was 6'5." However, I had spent my entire life guarding people bigger than me. I never played against anyone smaller than me so this challenge was something I had faced before. Defensively, we wanted to make the person we were guarding turn their back to create steal opportunities. Offensively, we wanted to keep the game at a snail's pace. However, because we had the speed advantage if Bobby Joe or I got a rebound, we were allowed to run up the court on a fast break. This could keep Kentucky off balance. Because there was not a shot clock, we could pass the ball as many times as we wanted, just like we did in practice, to control the tempo. And at the same time, they still had to guard against our speed.

When the ball was thrown in the air to start the game, history was made. But did we want to make history by losing a championship game? Pat Riley, the Hall of Fame Coach of the Lakers, Knicks, and Heat, was one of the star players for Kentucky. He was one of two All-Americans on Kentucky, along with Louie Dampier, and certainly a focus for us on defense. I cannot say enough nice things about Pat Riley. I have now known Pat for close to fifty years, and I can tell you he is a true gentleman and someone I have the utmost respect for, on and off the court. Pat hit the opening tip off to his teammate, but because he hit it on the way up, Texas Western gained control and took the ball out of bounds.

During our first possession, I was fouled by Larry Conley. And that's when I made some personal history. I missed the first foul shot of the 1966 N.C.A.A. championship game. I was not discouraged. I was going to shoot again before the night was over. Pat Riley then got the ball under our net and was fouled by David Lattin. He hit his second foul shot and Kentucky took the lead.

The next offensive series, even though it was so early in the game, was one of the most important parts of the game. David Lattin got the ball inside and threw down a monstrous dunk over defender Pat Riley. David hit his foul shot and we had a 3-1 lead, but that dunk did more than put points on the board. Pat Riley has been interviewed, graciously, about this game many times. He points out that after that dunk, he knew we were playing for something bigger than just a basketball game. Kentucky players, both in the game and on the bench, knew we were for real after that play. All the hype about us being the heavy underdogs seemed to go out the window when that three point play was complete.

Nine's were wild. Nine minutes into the game, the score was tied 9-9. However, when you are a heavy underdog in the media a tie game means you have the momentum.

Nevil Shed hit a free throw and we took the lead 10-9. That's when another important early game sequence took place.

Tommy Kron took the ball into our zone and I was guarding him. I sealed him off against the sideline and he had nowhere to go. Bobby Joe came across, stole the ball from him, and took it down the court for an easy lay up. After the score, Tommy Kron inbounded the ball to Louie Dampier. As Dampier crossed mid-court, he tried to make a move on Bobby Joe. When he turned, Bobby Joe picked his pocket and took the ball down for another easy lay up. Consecutive steals resulted in points for us. And just how David's dunk discouraged star player Pat Riley, my gut is that Bobby Joe's steal did the same thing to Louie Dampier. The body language on Kentucky's bench showed that they thought they were in trouble. We were winning 14-9, but it seemed like we had much more than a five point lead. When we took the lead 20-13, the difference in attitude between the two benches was even more obvious. We were showing enthusiasm, encouraging each other with each point and good play, while Kentucky was mostly sitting while staying very low key.

I hit a twenty foot jump shot and we were up 24-18. David hit two free throws and we took an eight point lead. When the score was 26-20, we took the ball down and set up our half court offense. I noticed Willie Cager open around the free throw line and got him the ball. He cut in between Kentucky's Thad Jaraz and Louie Dampier and finished with a huge dunk over Pat Riley. A dunk counts as two points just like any other field goal, but the physicality of it adds some important spice to it.

Tommy Kron hit a shot for Kentucky and the score was 28-23. I was unhappy that they scored, but also felt good that I had been assigned to guard Kron and these were his first points of the game.

Halftime came and we were winning by three points, 32-29. You can probably predict how Coach Haskins reacted to our first half performance. He stormed into the locker room, with a program rolled up in his hand, and chewed us out. "If you keep playing like this, you are going to lose!" "We need to rebound better! We need to play better defense! We need to apply more pressure!" The funny thing is that even though we were winning, I think everyone on the team agreed with Coach Haskins. We didn't feel like we were playing up to our potential. We could have done a better job in all the areas Coach Haskins mentioned. We knew we had somewhat contained their star players in Riley and Dampier, but if they got hot in the second half we could be in trouble. We left the locker room for the second half determined to play better. We were halfway home to a national championship. We could not let this game slip through our fingers.

Kentucky came out of the locker room determined as well. I'm sure Adolf Rupp, with all his years of coaching dominance at the collegiate level, set a fire under his players. With 16:50 left, Kentucky pulled within one point with the score 39-38. The battle was on.

I got hold of a deflected pass and kicked the ball out to Orsten Artis and we went up 41-38. Kentucky came down the court and missed their shot. It seemed like everyone on both teams scrambled for the rebound, and the call was jump ball. Kentucky's player for the jump ball was 6'4," and the Texas Western player was 5'6." It was me versus Pat Riley. Pat jumped high in the air towards the ball. I jumped in the air towards Pat's body. When you play at my height, you need to know every trick in the book. When we came down together I was able to tip the ball away from the off balance Riley and we controlled the ball.

As the game progressed, Kentucky continued to foul us. Two of their starters had four fouls and were now on the bench. When I hit two free throws, the first swirling around the rim for what felt like an eternity, we took a 52-45 lead. And for a team that couldn't shoot, we were doing a great job. At this point we hit sixteen of our eighteen free throw opportunities, and this was hugely important. When Pat Riley hit a jumper to cut our lead to 52-47, it was his first points in ten minutes. The stress Coach Haskins had put on defense all year was yielding results.

After a Bobby Joe Hill steal and score, we took a 58-51 lead. After a missed Kentucky shot, we moved the ball down the court and a shot was fired. It missed, but David Lattin went up in the air slammed home a ferocious dunk to put us up by nine points. Several minutes later, I hit a shot and we went up 62-54. Time was starting to become a factor for Kentucky if they were going to win.

With 3:06 left in the game, we were up 68-57. We were chewing up clock and hitting shots, and Kentucky had no choice but to quickly get off as many shots as they could. With 2:06 left, David Lattin hit an easy layup and we were winning 71-61. Kentucky starters were fouling out of the game, leaving to huge applause by the crowd.

With forty seconds left in the game, we were winning 71-63. I had the ball and ran around the court as fast as I could, trying to take time off the clock, knowing what was so close yet so far. I finally passed the ball and a foul was called. With less than twenty seconds left, Bobby Joe was open one on one against Pat Riley. Bobby Joe went for a shot and Pat fouled him. Pat Riley immediately initiated a handshake, which Bobby Joe accepted. Pat was letting Bobby Jo know that the foul was not in anyway poor sportsmanship, and knowing Pat I know that it was not. I also think he was congratulating Bobby Joe on a great game and for what was about to happen for our team. Bobby Joe hit one of his free throws. Louie Dampier came down the court and put a shot in the net, but the game was already decided. Kentucky scored first and last in the game, but we scored a heck of a lot in between. Several Kentucky players keeled over on the court stunned as the clock finally hit zero. The final score was 72-65. I was a surprise starter, but I played every minute of the game.

We won the game. I was dumbfounded. At the time, I didn't realize the magnitude of what just happened. Any collegiate championship is an amazing accomplishment, but ours had some added flavor. Records in sports are made to be broken, but when you are the first to do something that is something that can't be surpassed. We were the first team to have an all-black starting five to win an N.C.A.A. Championship. As I got older and could more fully realize the importance of that fact, this moment is certainly one of the treasured memories of my life. As we got enveloped in a sea of people, I had flashbacks of the 1963 High School Championship game at Madison Square Garden and my brother-in-law Gene running on the court to congratulate me.

Nevil Shed was always such a joyful, happy person who could always find a silly way to make you laugh. So when I saw him frantically trying to get my attention, I immediately wondered what he was up to now. If you are a basketball fan, you know that it is a tradition to cut down the nets after winning a championship. At the time, I didn't realize this because it was the first time I saw a championship game. The arena usually has a ladder ready for the winning team. But after we won, there wasn't a ladder in sight. Nevil had an idea. Since I was the smallest player on the team, he hoisted me on his shoulders and instructed me to take down the net. I didn't have scissors, so I undid the loops the best I could. I was worried that Nevil was not going to be able to hold me up for too much longer and my big night was going to end with a trip to the emergency room. We succeeded. The net was ours.

Through the years, people have asked me about the fact that a ladder was not taken out for our team. Sometimes I will joke and say that they must have seen me dunk a basketball and figured I could just fly up there if I wanted. Sometimes I joke that the arena workers must have placed the ladder behind the Kentucky bench and then forgot where they put it. In reality, I'm glad this happened.

My mother almost didn't let me go to El Paso. She let me go because I had big friends there, and Nevil was one of them. When a ladder was missing, he became my ladder. And because of his actions, any time you see video of us winning the championship you will see me taking down the net. Nevil's actions eventually got me on the cover of a Wheaties box, an honor among athletes. When I was young, my mother Julia was my ladder. If I needed something, even if it was difficult to attain, she was going to make sure I got there. My wife Claudia has been a ladder in my life. She has helped me elevate my life, our lives, in so many ways because of the sacrifices she made for our family. My daughters, Etta and Roz, are ladders of my life. Their beauty and love, throughout my life, has made me know that I can do anything in this world. My grandchildren are a ladder in my life. Each day, as I head towards my eventual retirement, they help to inspire me to keep working hard so I can eventually watch them achieve great things and reach the highest heights. I could write a book just talking about people who have helped me, and hopefully, whom I have helped as well.

When you have the beautiful family I do, in combination with the amazing friends I've made in my journey of life, you don't need a ladder to take down the net.

Chapter 10: The Beauty of the Good

"Don't waste yourself in rejection, nor bark against the bad, but chant the beauty of the good." Ralph Waldo Emerson.

    On June 26th, 2014, in an effort to help me write this book, I watched the March 19th, 1966 game film of the Texas Western versus Kentucky Championship game. I had not watched the game in decades, and I think the last time I tried I fell asleep. From a basketball standpoint, you could make an argument that it was a boring game. With no shot clock, we passed the ball around so much the scorer's table could have used a sun dial for the official time. Our methodical approach on offense and defense was not exactly the run and gun style that excites crowds nowadays. Now I watch the game through the eyes of a high school basketball coach and I don't love the way I played. I see little things here and there I could have done better, and I wonder if I would have taken myself out of the game. Don Haskins, my Hall of Fame Coach, might disagree with that assessment since he had me play every minute of the game.
    However, watching the game on this beautiful afternoon was special. In fact, it is a memory I will treasure forever because of who I watched it with. The apples of my eye,
my daughter Roz and granddaughters Brianana, 17, and twins Kayla and Mahogany, 11, were with me. Knowing how smart they all are and how much I value their opinions, I was curious about their observations. Besides the pride that I know they all feel for my accomplishments in winning a National Championship, it was interesting to notice some of the subtle slights that they picked up on in the video. I think for all four of them, growing up in another generation than I did, it was surprising in some sense. Kayla and Mahogany both commented that it seemed as if the announcer of the game was a fan of Kentucky. Announcers are really just supposed to relay the action taking place, whereas they both felt that he'd get excited when Kentucky made a good play and less excited when we did something right. Brianana noticed that the word "showboating" was used in reference to Texas Western, but never for one of the Kentucky players. Why was that? Roz felt like the announcers focused more on what Kentucky was doing wrong as opposed to what we were doing right. We were fifteen for seventeen at the free throw line that night, and that is what won us the game. However, instead of pointing that out it seemed like Kentucky was getting credit for hitting more field goals than we did. Adolph Rupp even mentioned that statistic in his post game press conference. Why does it matter who made more field goals in a game that we won by seven points? We laughed

together that day about how I looked as my granddaughters pointed out that my walk hasn't changed in forty-eight years. We laughed every time I traveled or missed a shot, and I saw them light up every time I scored a point or made a good play. But their instincts about the game were very astute. Not everyone in the world was happy that Texas Western won that game.

On March 19th, 1966, after I took down the nets, without the help of a ladder, it was time for the trophy presentations. Before we received our championship trophy, they announced the winner of the tournament M.V.P. That honor went to Utah's Jerry Chambers. Jerry did have a great tournament and was an incredible player. However, most sports fans reading this book would probably agree with me that the M.V.P. of a World Series, Super Bowl, N.B.A. or N.C.A.A. championship usually comes from the winning team. Jerry Chambers last played in the tournament consolation game. In my mind, Bobby Joe Hill should have been named the M.V.P. As important as David Lattin's dunk was in the beginning of the game, Bobby Joe's two steals put us ahead for good. The backlash for the first all-black starting five to win a championship was almost immediate.

A tradition at the time was for the winning N.C.A.A. team to be guests on the Ed Sullivan Show. We were not invited. I guess it's possible that we got bumped for The Beatles if they were in town, but I have a gut feeling there might have been another reason why. The funny thing is I didn't even care about being on the show, but there was a reason I wanted to get the invitation. It would have been a free trip to New York City for me to see my mother, Claudia, my beautiful Etta, and the rest of my family and friends.

Over the course of time, stories started to crop up in the media with a very negative spin on Texas Western and our sports program. There is a John Updike poem called "Ex-Basketball Player" about a great high school baller named Flick. Flick is a star, but once he leaves school he has nothing:

> "He never learned a trade, he just sells gas
> Checks Oil, and changes flats.
> Once in a while
> As a gag, he dibbles an inner tube
> But most of us remember anyway
> His hands are fine and nervous on the lug wrench
> It makes no difference to the lug wrench, though"

This was the theme of some of the stories that started to come in about us. People were implying that the black players on our team only had basketball skills and left El Paso unprepared for life. People started to believe that we were like mercenaries, brought in from around the country to take down Kentucky. Part of me feels like the motive to do this was to diminish our victory, not out of any genuine concern for the well being of the black Texas Western players. If we didn't really belong as students at Texas Western, our win over the white lineup of Kentucky should have been null and void. And this belief was not just limited to the white community. People in the black community started to believe what they were hearing and negativity from them started to trickle in as well. For the most part, Don Haskins felt the brunt of negativity from the black community. They felt he exploited us and threw us aside when he got what he wanted, a National Championship. I can tell you that these things were simply not true.

    The first thing Don Haskins ever said to me when I came to El Paso was about my schoolwork. He told me how important it was and he didn't even mention basketball. Coach Haskins set up regular study hours that were monitored. When some of the athletes, black and white, tried to pretend they were studying by wearing sunglasses and sleeping at their desks, he ran us to death for it. Did Don Haskins recruit players because of their basketball ability? Of course he did. So did Adolf Rupp and probably every other coach who has ever walked onto a collegiate court. That doesn't mean he didn't care about us as people or whether or not we were studying. I don't know the grade point averages of my friends or have access to their transcripts, but here are some important facts about our team. I have a Bachelors of Science in Management. I have had a non-basketball related career for the past forty-five years. Harry Flournoy and Willie Cager both became high school teachers. David Lattin, after playing professional basketball, got a Bachelors of Science degree in Business Administration. Bobby Joe Hill became the Vice-President of El Paso Natural Gas. Nevil Shed worked as a coordinator for Student Activities at the University of Texas at San Antonio and Orsten Artis became a police detective in his native Gary, Indiana. For all of us the college education that we received at Texas Western, which was not as common for minority students as it is today, created a foundation that led to many successful endeavors and career opportunities. For a bunch of kids that were being used, we didn't do too badly for ourselves.

    I write about some of the negativity surrounding our win as a way of reporting history, and not because these are things that have been eating away at me for years. I always like to say "my haters are my motivators." In my heart I knew the truth about what we did in El Paso and that's all I will ever need. My style is to focus on the beauty and good in a situation and there was plenty of that going around once the final buzzer sounded against Kentucky.

    It's hard to describe how important I felt when the airplane touched down at the El Paso airport. As we got off the plan, we were greeted by a sea of screaming fans. It was the people from the community coming out to show us love and respect. And it was a melting pot – black fans, white fans,

Mexican fans. Race didn't matter to them. They were Texas Western Miners fans and we were all one cohesive group. It was almost like they felt that the city of El Paso had all of a sudden magically appeared on all the maps in the world. They gave us a ticker tape parade from the airport to the school campus. I rode alone in a convertible and waved to fans cheering me the entire trip. And I can tell you this; no one could force me to sit in the middle here if I didn't want to.

The next day, the team met in the school gym. It was almost like an exit meeting. We cleared out some of our stuff and met with the team trainer to discuss any injuries, etc. Coach Haskins read us a telegram that he received. It was from Bill Cosby and it was addressed to Coach Haskins and the Texas Western Miners. It read "Thank you for the most enjoyable victory I have ever witnessed. An underdog team that came on and played with class and confidence -- Bill Cosby" As a black entertainer finding success in an industry mostly dominated by whites, I think he had a special appreciation for what we accomplished. This was huge to me. A celebrity thinking about us almost made me feel like a celebrity myself.

On March 28th, 1966, *Sports Illustrated* published its newest issue. I was on the cover. The main focus of the cover picture showed Harry Flournoy under the net wrestling a rebound away from Pat Riley. I am in the background close to the foul line reacting to the play. When I first saw the cover, I was happy that Harry's foot didn't block me in the picture. His foot only blocks my shoulders so you can see my face and my number as well. I am so happy that of all the players, Harry made the cover. He badly hurt his knee in the middle of the championship game and could not return. As our captain, he was so important to our team success, my personal success, and I'm glad he got this recognition. Harry and his wife Sukari are still, to this day, some of the dearest friends I have in the world.

Sports Illustrated at that time cost thirty-five cents and I did not buy the issue. I know people sometimes don't believe me when I tell them that, but I swear it is true. People who have not been touched by poverty might not have the appreciation of how much every penny counts. If I could buy a magazine describing something I witnessed first hand or put two delicious chili dogs in my hungry belly, the chili dogs would win every time. However, I have been told about the content of the article by many people who have a copy of the issue. In the article, there is no mention of us being the first all-black starting five to win an N.C.A.A. Championship. I always found that to be interesting and believe you can look at it two different ways. It's possible that the events were reported without focusing on the race issue, the way it would be covered nowadays. Or it's possible that what we accomplished was not something to be advertised. I guess we will never know. Many of the students on campus picked up a copy of the magazine as a souvenir. In fact, so many people bought the issue that the school set up tables on campus for Harry and me to sign copies for anyone who wanted. I felt honored that so many of my fellow students wanted my autograph enough to wait in a long line to get it.

    A couple of days after the championship game, another student knocked on my dorm room door. I had a phone call. I walked to the pay phone in the hall and was shocked to hear who was on the other end. It was my father. We had not spoken or seen each other in a very long time. I was blown away. He saw the game on television and he wanted to tell me how proud he was. His son was a winner. And even though he was on some level out of my life, it never meant that he was out of my heart. I loved him. The call didn't restart our relationship. In fact, it's possible that it was the last time we spoke. But because we won against Kentucky, I was given once last chance to connect with my Dad. That phone call was beauty. That phone call was good.

Chapter 11: Last Year and Next Year

*"For last year's words belong to last year's language
And next year's words await another voice
And to make an end is to make a beginning"*
--Ralph Waldo Emerson

In the fall of 1966, it was time for Texas Western to get back to playing basketball. We were the defending champions. However, just as is the case for all college teams, we did not have the exact same lineup. Our roster included David Lattin, Nevil Shed, David Palacio, Togo Railey, Dick Myers, Fred Carr, Gary Crowell, Tony Harper, Phil Harris, Kerry John, and of course, Willie Worsley. There were some important names missing from this list.

Harry Flournoy and Orsten Artis were the captains of our championship team but, as seniors, they had graduated and moved on. Leadership in a locker room is something that can be overlooked in sports. People see what happens on the court, but don't always realize the importance of team leaders; Harry and Orsten were exceptional team leaders. Following their lead and emulating their maturity always helped me when I was an underclassman on the team. In addition to the loss of Harry and Orsten, Bobby Joe did not return to the team. I have described the easy going attitude Bobby Joe had towards everything, and that included basketball. Even though he was such a natural, and I have no doubt he would have been a successful professional player, it's possible that basketball just wasn't his passion. We were champions. We had nothing left to prove. In a way, I think the love for his future wife Tina was his passion and he may have realized that spending his final year at school with her would have made him much happier than running sprints and doing all the work the basketball season would have required. Bobby marched to the beat of his own drummer and that is one of the many things I loved about the man.

With Bobby Joe and Orsten gone, I now stepped into the role of the number one guard. This was a challenge. I love challenges, but this one made my junior season much tougher than my sophomore year. Other teams now keyed on me. I was now usually guarded by the opponent's top defensive player, so I had to work even harder to set up my teammates with passes. And even though I was a natural shooter, I had to really fight for every point I scored. David Lattin and Willie Cager were still playing well as big men, but we did not dominate the way we did the previous season. However, Don Haskins, as always, did a masterful coaching job and we still finished a very respectable 22-6. At that time, I considered twenty wins the yardstick of a good season.

Because we were the defending champions, there was no sneaking up on teams the way we had the previous season. Every team probably wrote our name on their calendar as a benchmark game. On the road, I think the crowds were bigger and more hostile than ever because if the home team could beat us it would have been huge. Whenever a team repeats championships in consecutive seasons, it is amazing to me. Success gets harder to attain instead of easier for champions.

At 22-6, we once again made the N.C.A.A. tournament. We flew to Corvalis, Oregon for a neutral site game against Seattle. However, because of Oregon's proximity to Seattle, and the various other reasons crowds seemed to root against us, it certainly did not feel "neutral" to us at all. It was a battle, but we were able to use our speed and defense to gut out a win. The final score was 62-54. For the second year in a row, we advanced to the sweet sixteen. We played a team called Pacific, whose campus was located in Northern California. What I didn't realize at the tip off of that game was that it would be the last meaningful post season game I would play as a collegiate athlete. Pacific was able to capitalize on our mistakes and we just couldn't seem to maintain enough pressure on both offense and defense. We lost the game 72-63 and were eliminated from the tournament. There would be no repeat. The magic that started on December 2, 1965 came to an end on March 17th, 1967. It was one heck of a ride.

In those days, they would play consolation games in the regional brackets. I'm not sure why. Maybe it was just another way to get fans into an arena and draw money at the gate. We were pitted against Wyoming, who also lost their playoff game. We won the game 69-67 and I do think that win says a lot for Coach Haskins and our squad. It would have been easy, after the disappointment of losing to Pacific, and especially after coming off a national championship, for us to phone it in. We didn't. Coach Haskins wouldn't let us, and we had too much pride and respect for the game of basketball to not take a game seriously when we walked onto the court.

When the tournament was over, a new champion was crowned. It's possible you've heard some of the names associated with the 1967 championship team. The school was U.C.L.A. The coach was John Wooden, considered by many to be the greatest basketball coach of all time. The M.V.P. of the tournament was Lew Alcindor; later known as Kareem-Abdul Jabbar. Lew Alcindor would win three consecutive tournament M.V.P. awards before going on to one of the most successful professional careers ever. Nowadays, someone as talented as Lew Alcindor might go straight from high school to the N.B.A. John Wooden coached seven consecutive championship teams starting with the one that succeeded Texas Western. Having experienced the momentous task of trying to repeat as champions, I think this record is the most impressive in the history of collegiate sports, and maybe all sports. Having played against Lew when we were in high school, it was good to see the legacy of New York City basketball, the religion of the streets of New York City, staying in the national limelight.

In the fall of 1967, I prepared for my final year of collegiate athletic eligibility. The school was now called The University of Texas at El Paso, UTEP, and this was a sign of how the school had grown in such a short amount of time. Our enrollment brought us from having college status to being a full-fledged university. Only Willie Cager and I remained from the team that had won the championship game versus Kentucky in March of 1966. We struggled. We finished with a record of 14-9 and didn't qualify for the N.C.A.A. tournament. Just like I felt when I lost the championship game at DeWitt Clinton my senior year, this was not the way I wanted things to end. However, there was one amazing bright spot for me that season. I got to share the backcourt with Nate "Tiny" Archibald.

If you are a basketball fan, the name Tiny Archibald should ring a bell. If not, I will tell you a little bit about one of my best friends in the world. In 1969, Tiny was a first-round draft pick of the Cincinnati Royals of the N.B.A. He played fourteen years in the league and in the early 1980's he won a championship ring with the Boston Celtics and their up-and-coming star, Larry Bird. He was elected to the Naismith Memorial Basketball Hall of Fame in 1991, and in 1996 he was voted one of the top fifty players to ever play the game as part of the N.B.A 50th Anniversary team. And with all that on his resume, my personal favorite piece of trivia about Tiny is that he is the only N.B.A. player to ever lead the league in scoring and assists in the same season. That is an amazing feat.

Tiny was about 6'1," 150 pounds. His nickname really didn't come from his size. His father went by "Tiny," so I think it was akin to calling him "Junior." Our relationship predated our time at El Paso. We both attended DeWitt Clinton High School together in the early 1960's. I was a couple of years older than Tiny and I tried to take him under my wing a little bit. Tiny is one of the smartest people I have ever met, but school is not for everyone. Tiny did not enjoy school and he did not take advantage of his academic potential. He may have been twice as smart as I was, but my grades were twice as good as his because I worked harder. I think Tiny's poor grades scared away colleges. He was so good he could have played anywhere, but he had to make a pit stop at a junior college before he could join me in El Paso.

If Bobby Joe could walk on water as a guard, Tiny could run on water. Tiny is the best player I have ever played with. He was left-handed, and even though another team might know he was going to make a move to his left, it didn't matter. He could not be stopped. And because I looked out for Tiny at Dewitt Clinton, I think he always looked out for me when we played together at El Paso. He could have been the leading scorer in every college game he ever played. However, he always made sure that I got my hands on the ball whenever he could get it to me. If he could pick one of us scoring, he would have picked me. There were times when I would win M.V.P. in a tournament and it was all because of Tiny. Since I was a senior, I think he wanted me to shine in my final season. He knew he had more years of eligibility and there would be plenty of time for him to get his points. It takes an amazing person to do something like that.

Tiny is quiet in nature, just like me. We might have said 100 words to each other all season, but that's because we didn't have to talk. We both knew how much love and mutual respect we had for each other. To this day, Tiny is one of my biggest supporters. When I am coaching a big game for Spring Valley High School, Tiny will stop by and root us on. And the funny thing is, even to this day, when I see Tiny, he always says the same thing to me. "Will, if I had listened to you in high school I would have been on that championship team." With all his accomplishments, there is still some disappointment in not having participated in that landmark event. Having Tiny in my life all these years has been nothing short of a blessing.

On April 4th, 1968, Martin Luther King Jr. was assassinated. I've always said that my mother was my "She ro" and if I had one person to choose as a hero, it would be Dr. King. My sophomore year of college, my first year on varsity, I played in a game that would eventually be looked at as a highlight of the civil rights movement of the 1960's. As I was getting ready to leave school, shortly after my final varsity game, I lived through the worst day in the history of the civil rights movement and in reality, the history of the United States. When I look back at that day, there is a part of me that gets a little mad at myself. At that time, I don't think I fully appreciated his message of turning the other cheek. Growing up in the Bronx, we did not turn the other cheek. If someone did something to me, I was forced to fight back. As I got older and wiser, I realized that he *was* fighting back. Martin Luther King was not afraid to die to prove his point to the world. In fact, I know in my heart that God touched him and told him to get ready. And of all things, that's what amazes me about this special man. I'm glad he was alive to receive his Nobel Peace Prize in 1964. I wish he would have gotten to see all the streets named after him throughout our country. It's a shame that we sometimes wait until people are gone to show our appreciation for them. I have been interviewed, coming up on five decades, about the role Texas Western played in the civil rights movement. I am proud of our accomplishments, but I also know that what we went through was not as difficult as what others endured. We were a team. We had several black players all going through the same experience together. Jackie Robinson had to go through things alone. He had the support of the team owner and some white players on his team, but he was still the only black player. Martin Luther King was not the only black man seeking justice in our country, but he was willing to stand at a podium alone, be the face of the movement, and he ultimately paid for it with his life.

I'm sure for a lot of seniors, finishing college can be bittersweet. I had made lifelong friends that I was not going to see as much. I saw myself grow as a person during my time in El Paso. And, of course, I had participated in a sporting event that would be talked about for decades to come.

I was majoring in Physical Education with an eye towards becoming a teacher. Because of my basketball schedule, though, I was never able to student teach and my plan was to finish that up in New York. I could not afford to come back to El Paso for another year, but I knew that I could use my credits from Texas Western to complete my degree closer to home with Claudia and Etta by my side. Then my life took an unexpected turn.

I was called down to the athletic office. I had no idea what was going on. The season was over. What did they want from me? When I got there, I was told I had a phone call. I picked up the receiver and what I was told was extremely shocking news. I swear it was something that was not even on my radar. Someone must have noticed the points I scored my senior year, largely due to Tiny taking care of me. Someone also must have noticed that I had a successful collegiate career.

I was told that I had been drafted by a team from the American Basketball Association, more commonly referred to as the A.B.A. Nine years earlier, I stood outside a chain link fence unable to get an invitation into a New York City pick-up game. Now I was getting an invitation to play professional basketball. Life gave me a head fake and drove hard to the hoop.

Chapter 12: The Gift

"...a significant event can be the catalyst for choosing a direction that serves us- and those around us- more effectively. Look for the learning."
-Louisa May Alcott.

    I was chosen in the final round of the 1968 A.B.A draft by the Dallas Chaparrals. And to this day, I have never bothered to ask anyone what the heck a Chaparral is. Being selected by Dallas stunned me and believe it or not, I was faced with a difficult decision. Initially, I was not sure if this was what I wanted to do moving forward.
    Since I was surprised by my selection, I started to ask myself why they picked me. Did they take me because I had made a name for myself in another Texas city, El Paso? In college, people used to come early to games to watch someone my size dunk a basketball. Was this why I was selected? Was Dallas using me as a sideshow to put some meat in the seats? This was only the second year that the American Basketball Association was in existence and most of the franchises were struggling with attendance problems and not coming close to the popularity of the N.B.A teams. I wanted to feel that I was being drafted because of my ability, not for the purpose of entertaining people during warm-ups.
    I talked it over with some of the people at El Paso and decided to report to camp with Dallas. Players get drafted for all different reasons, and maybe I shouldn't overanalyze my selection too much. At that time, I knew of high school teachers getting paid 6,000 dollars a year. How could I pass up the offer of 9,000 dollars a year, with checks coming in on the first and fifteenth of every month? I would be getting paid to play the sport that I had loved for most of my life, and 9,000 dollars a year at the time felt like LeBron James money!
    My time with Dallas was brief. After two weeks of training camp, the general manager of the team told me I had been traded. I was surprised. I felt that I had been playing well during the team practices and scrimmages. In a way, it was the first time I felt rejected in regards to basketball since the time I was cut from the Dewitt Clinton High School team my sophomore year. However, there was some great news about the trade. I was shipped to the New York Nets. When I heard the words New York, my heart almost broke through my chest. I could play close to home and be with Claudia and Etta full time. I really felt like things were falling into place. I packed up my gear and returned home. The A.B.A season would start in the fall and I had some weeks off before I had to report to the Nets training camp.
    During the summer of 1968, I stayed in basketball shape by playing in the famous Rucker Park Basketball Tournament. Rucker Park is located on

155th street and 8th Avenue in Manhattan. The park is named after Holcombe Rucker, who started the summer tournaments in the 1950's as a spotlight for children of poverty to show off their skills. Eventually, it became a rite of passage for players all around the country. Here, I played against some of the all-time greats. I faced Wilt Chamberlain, Kareem Abdul Jabbar, Bill Bradley, Connie Hawkins, Austin Carr, Dave Collins, and "Dr. J." Julius Erving. I also got to play again with some of my friends for life, like Nate "Tiny" Archibald, Willie Cager, and Nevil Shed. For younger basketball fans reading this book, people like Kobe Bryant and Lebron James have also come to play at Rucker Park and keep its legacy alive. One year at a Rucker Park tournament, I won an award for sportsmanship. I am very proud of that. As I mentioned earlier, I have never received a technical foul.

Playing in the Rucker Park tournaments has meant a lot to me. I held my own against some of the greatest N.B.A players of all-time. And in my heart, knowing how well I performed there, I believe that if I was six inches taller, I would have been drafted into the N.B.A and have had a successful career. I promise that I say this not from a place of bitterness. Being bitter about things beyond my control is just not the type of person I am. However, I would have loved to have gotten a shot to prove what I could do on the biggest basketball stage in the world. Unfortunately for me, people my height just were not drafted into the N.B.A at that time.

A week before I was to report for the Nets, during a Rucker Park game, I received a vicious elbow to the head. My eye closed up and I looked like a boxer who needed to get cut so he could come out for the next round. I got twelve stitches and I had to wear a patch that made me look like a pirate. I was very worried that this might hurt my chances of making the team. Luckily for me, the swelling went down enough before my tryout. I had a good workout and the coaches were impressed. I made the team. I was officially a professional basketball player.

My coach with the New York Nets was Max Zaslofsky. Max, at one time, had been a shooting guard for the Knicks, and since that was my position, I think he took a liking to me. I think the fact that I was a New York boy myself didn't hurt either. It was important that Max liked me because shooting guards are a dime a dozen. As much as basketball has changed over the years, in a lot of ways it is still the same: you have to put the ball in their basket and you have to stop people from putting the ball in your basket. There are only so many big guys in the world, so height and size are always at a premium. There were probably a million guys my size that could shoot a ball. I knew I had to take advantage of the opportunity I was getting.

Overall, I liked Max as a coach. The training camp he ran was physically demanding, but the practices we had once the season started were much different from what I was used to at El Paso. At El Paso, we were run to death. For the Nets, practices were more like a walk-through on offense and defense. This was mostly because we traveled more in the pros. We conserved our energy during the season and didn't have as much time to practice as we did during the long stretches on campus at El Paso.

In some ways, the rules of the A.B.A. catered to a shooter of my size. The A.B.A introduced the three point shot into basketball. The N.B.A would not adopt this rule until the two leagues merged several years later. Because of the three point shot, I could work from the outside, stay away from the big guys beating each other up in the paint, get my points, and help my team. When I first started playing with the ball my mother gave me for Christmas years earlier, I worked on shooting from the edges of the jump ball circle. This was paying off for me now. I was one of the best three point shooters in the league.

Another thing often associated with the A.B.A. is the red, white, and blue ball. The A.B.A was looking for ways to differentiate itself from the N.B.A, and someone must have figured that a different colored ball would do just that. I know a lot of players that did not like the different ball, but I did. Some said they didn't like the feel of the new ball, but the seams were wider than and N.B.A ball and because of this, I could palm it. This gave me a feeling of more control. When a shooter is hot, he or she has a good, steady rotation on the ball. I found that because of the difference in colors on an A.B.A ball, I could visually make out the rotation better and it helped me shoot.

The home court of the New York Nets, in 1968, was located in Commack, Long Island. Living in The Bronx, I would hop on a train and meet the team trainer in Queens. He would then drive me out to games. The arena in Commack was actually a rink for hockey, so before basketball games they would put down a portable court over the ice. This made for terrible playing conditions. The floor was always slippery. Not only that, but the floor would have dead spots. Dead spots on a basketball court mean that the ball doesn't bounce back properly. There were so many areas like this in the A.B.A. arenas that players were basically allowed to palm the ball and move it over dead spots without traveling being called. This wasn't an official rule; it was unwritten, but the referees had to look the other way or our games would have never ended.

Attendance for our games was not good. On any given night, we might have between 300 and 500 people in the stands. As the Spring Valley high school basketball coach, I have seen us draw more people than that many times. Team owners were trying anything to get people to turn out. There always seemed to be a gadget giveaway here, or a discount hot dog night there. Nothing seemed to work. The league was struggling financially.

On January 5th, 1969, we played the New Orleans Buccaneers. I felt I had a good game in our losing effort. It was my last game as a professional basketball player. The next day, Max and someone from the Nets management told me the team was releasing me. They promised me it had nothing to do with my ability, attitude, or how I was playing. In fact, they basically guaranteed that another team would claim me on waivers. The move was an economic one. My contract was not guaranteed, unlike those of most of the other players on the team. If they released some of those guys, they would still have to pay them. If they released me at this point of the season, before I reached a certain number of games, they would not have to pay me. I was the easiest person, from an economic and paperwork standpoint, to cut. It's amazing to think that my life changed because not enough people came to "Buy One, Get One Free Hot Dog Night!"

For close to a decade, basketball had been such a huge part of my life. On the streets of The Bronx, it offered me a positive outlet in a tough neighborhood. It got me friends on the playgrounds. It gave me self-esteem and direction in high school. It got me a college education. But on this day, I saw a side of basketball that I had never clearly seen before. It was a business, and even though I was playing well it didn't matter to the bottom line. The numbers in the budget didn't add up and for me, out of the blue, the business of basketball was officially closed.

My daughter Roz has always been my protector. She tells me the truth. She puts me in my place when I need it and her straightforward personality is always true and genuine. I wanted to name her Willamina after me, but Claudia wouldn't have it. It didn't matter. Naming her after me would not have made her any more a part of me than she already is. We even look alike. When she was a toddler, people started calling her "Little Willie" because of our resemblance. We think alike. We have so many similarities in personality that it is almost scary. Roz is not a sentimental person. She does not throw around "I love you" the way some people do without meaning it. But we don't need words to express our love. We know it is there, so we don't need to say it. I am so proud of the amazing person she is. In addition to being an amazing daughter, Roz is a wonderful mother. As an aunt, she has extended herself to help out with Etta's kids as well. She even volunteers her time in the community working with young people as a coach. The world is a better place because of Roz.

Roz got her brains from her mother and her athletic ability from me. And believe it or not, I originally tried to discourage her from playing basketball. I always thought that there would be too many comparisons to me and that this might put undue pressure on her, but basketball was in her blood and eventually, it was game on. At some point in her early years, I was her coach. I was tough on her and there were times when a game was over that she didn't even want to talk to me. I was tough out of love. I saw her potential and wanted to make her the best player she could be. Nowadays, I think Roz has the same problem coaching her daughters Mahogany and

Kayla. It is difficult to serve in the dual role as parent and coach, but I figured that if she could get through me, she could play against anyone.

In 8th grade, Roz won a New York State foul shooting championship. You would have never known, because she never brags about anything. She calmly came home and placed the trophy in her room like it was nothing. I think she hit twenty three out of twenty five shots in the final round to take the title. There are plenty of N.B.A players who would kill to shoot like that. In 1983, Roz was a freshman and played basketball for her high school team. She attended an all-girls private school in New Jersey called Immaculate Heart Academy. I don't think the all-girls element worked for her, so the next year she attended a co-ed school, Albertus Magnus in Bardonia, New York. Here, Roz thrived academically and in athletics. In basketball, she was all-county, all-league, and eventually received a scholarship to play for the University of Lowell, located in Massachusetts. Once again, a Worsley was finding success on a collegiate court. Roz was her team's leading scorer. She was once named East Coast player of the week, and the East Coast included schools from Maine to Florida. When Roz arrived at Lowell, the school's basketball program was struggling. By the time Roz graduated, she held eighteen school records, Lowell won a league championship, and she was invited to try out for the U.S.A Olympic team.

Roz was born on January 8th, 1969, two days after I was released by the New York Nets, and I know in my heart that Roz was a very specific gift from God, given to me when I needed it most. Instead of being devastated that my basketball life seemed to be coming to a close, this was one of the happiest times of my life. I had another beautiful woman in my life. I think I knew our family was complete and it was now me, Claudia, Etta and Roz -- ready to take on the world. As a father of a newborn, I didn't have time to wallow in self-pity. I had to change diapers, make bottles, and focus in on the most important thing in life -- family. In many ways, through Roz, my life and legacy in basketball has never gone away. However, at the same time, the birth of Roz made me realize something else as well. Maybe basketball wasn't my true calling in life. Maybe I was meant to do something else in this world. I needed a new career and decided that I wanted to work in human services. I wanted a career in which I could work helping others, and that is what I have done since Roz came into my life. I like to think that more people have benefitted from my career change than would have from watching me play basketball. As I mentioned, Roz always protects me and steers me in the right direction. The funny thing is, she started doing that from the second she was born. My beautiful Roz!

Chapter 13: Dreams Do Come True

"When your dreams include service to others- accomplishing something that contributes to others- it also accelerates the accomplishment of that goal. People want to be part of something that contributes and makes a difference."
- Jack Canfield

If I was given the choice of hitting the game winning shot in a basketball game 365 days a year, or helping someone who needs it 365 days a year, there really would be no dilemma for me. As great a feeling as it is to succeed in athletics, it pales in comparison, for me, to the feeling of improving the life of another human being. Most people would probably assume that my dream job would have been being a professional basketball player longer, but that really would have been my second choice. My dream job was always to be a social worker. I feel like social workers do God's work. However, in the winter of 1969, with a wife and two young daughters, going back to school for a degree in social work was not an option. Fortunately for me, I was blessed to find a job that was similar to social work, yet allowed me to start right away, and I know in my heart that this led me towards my true calling in life.

I was hired at a residential facility in the Bronx called Woodycrest, because it was located on Woodycrest Avenue. From a logistics standpoint, it was perfect. I was so close to our apartment that I could walk to work. Claudia was working as a secretary part time each day from 8 A.M. to noon. My hours at Woodycrest were from 1 P.M. to 9 P.M., so we were able to rotate taking care of Etta and Roz while still making enough money to get by.

Woodycrest provided services for people who were emotionally disturbed or in distress. Many of these young people came from broken homes and were placed in Woodycrest by the court system. Many of them were classified as P.I.N.S., which stands for Persons in Need of Supervision. I think the fact that I was only twenty-three years old at the time, and also a product of a single-parent home, helped me relate to these kids in a special way.

My first job with Woodycrest was as Recreational Director. I was charged with finding activities to keep students busy and out of trouble. Because of my background as an athlete, along with all the courses in physical education that I took at Texas Western, I gravitated towards sports as our focus. In essence, I organized gym classes. The facility had access to a pool, so I would take everyone there and try to help them improve as swimmers. I organized basketball games and eventually we started a team. I reached out to other similar facilities in the city and we ended up competing against them. It was a great way to teach teamwork, discipline, and camaraderie. From July to September, I worked with the Woodycrest sleep away camp in Bear Mountain, New York. People who have never lived in a major city might not be able to appreciate what it means to go from the city to the beautiful fresh air of the country, even just for a day. The students really enjoyed the summer camp and it was a great experience for me as well.

I have such fond memories of Etta and Roz, my little girls, bonding together as I started my new career. Etta, four years older than Roz, was already showing the qualities that make a great parent. She would give Roz her bottle and treat her like a little china doll. Roz used to love to wear clothes, but always hated wearing diapers. She would tear them off, put on any clothes, or hat, that she could find, and run around our apartment. Roz, as an adult, is a person that is always on the go and things were no different even when she was a toddler. But even with all the happy times we had in our first apartment, Claudia thought it might be time for us to move. We moved to a northern section of the Bronx, getting an apartment at 920 White Plains Road. My mother Julia instilled a strong work ethic in me and I didn't take a vacation my first three years at Woodycrest. This helped us save up enough money not only for our move, but also for a car to get me back and forth to work. From someone who came from such poverty in the South, I felt a lot of pride buying a Duster with white wall tires, an AM/FM radio, and air conditioning.

In 1974, Woodycrest once again gave me an amazing career opportunity. Woodycrest and another residential facility named Happy Valley were merging. The joint campus was in Pomona of Rockland County. Impressed with the work I was doing, they offered me a promotion to Residential Director of the new campus and I accepted. Claudia and I could not pass up the chance to raise our girls in this beautiful suburb less than an hour outside of New York City. As Residential Director, my family was given nice apartment housing on campus and we felt like this was ideal for us. If we were ever going to be able to move from the city, this was our shot.

In a relatively short amount of time, I went from organizing activities to overseeing about ninety employees. There were one or two people above me, but I was in charge of all the day-to-day functions. This was a twenty-four hour a day job because I was always on call. I made the schedule and rotated the different counselors in charge, but if anything major ever happened, I would always be called in. If a fight happened at four in the morning, I would get a phone call at 4:01 A.M. I'm not complaining about that. I loved this job. With my desire to do social work and help others, this job gave me the opportunity to touch the lives of many young people who needed it. Even though the Woodycrest campus was now in Rockland County, the young people living there were still almost all from the city. When Woodycrest was in the Bronx, it was easy for students to leave and get home. They could leave the campus and hop on a bus or subway and be home in minutes. The thinking behind moving the campus outside the city was that it would be impossible for students to leave. This was not the case. Students who really wanted to leave would find a way to jump on a bus and make it to the Port Authority in Manhattan. However, this did not happen often. My gut feeling is that most of the students at Woodycrest came to appreciate their new situation and, for me, that was very gratifying.

Even though I was out of basketball, basketball was not completely out of me. When we still lived in the Bronx, I would play at Rucker Park or in local pick up games. Etta and Roz would come watch me play and were exposed to sports at a very young age. Etta would calmly sit in the stands and wait for the games to end. Roz, from the time she could walk, would come down from the bleachers and try to join a team. As my girls got older, their time living on the campus of Woodycrest would further their interest, and abilities, in sports.

Etta's catchphrase as a little girl was, "I don't sweat, I perspire," and that is not the usual motto of a deeply committed athlete. However, being older and taller than Roz, she was able to play some defense. The challenge of overcoming Etta's age and size advantages certainly made Roz a better offensive player in the years to come. One day, Etta accidently hit Roz with an elbow and gave her a bloody lip. It was unintentional, but I think that event stunted Etta's interest in sports. Etta loved Roz so much that I think the thought of hurting her made her shy away from the contact needed to play basketball. Years later, Etta would eventually play basketball for Canton Junior College. She had height, and athletic ability in her blood, but she was the last person on the bench. This didn't bother her at all. Years later I would find out that, knowing she wasn't going to play, Etta would wear pajamas under her sweat suit so she could go right to bed after the game. She did not have passion for sports the way me and Roz did.

With Etta drifting away from an interest in sports, Roz needed new athletic challenges and she found that in the kids at Woodycrest. Since we were living there, she became friendly with many of the students. Roz was quiet like me and a lot of the students took her under their wings and were very protective of her. The respect that the students had for me filtered down to my children. Woodycrest students were from the city and, as I said, basketball is the religion of the city. Take it from me, these kids could play. Even though she was breathing in nice country air, Roz was getting the same New York City basketball education that I got years earlier.

Softball was a big activity at Woodycrest and that became Roz's next sporting love. She played in the campus games and on Sunday mornings I would spend hours hitting her the ball and pitching to her. When Roz eventually decided she wanted to pitch, she was a natural. Roz was so strong that she didn't even need to throw the ball windmill the way most people do. She would just whip the ball around her body and get the same velocity as everyone else. Roz eventually became an all-star in an all-girls Spring Valley little league. She even threw a no-hitter. When she got older, she was a standout player at Albertus Magnus High School in Bardonia.

In 1992, Woodycrest closed and I went to work for a facility named Lakeside, which eventually was renamed Evan Gould. Again, I was hired as Resident Director and I took on much of the same responsibilities that I had had at Woodycrest. I worked at Residential Facilities for close to twenty-five years and my time at each one provided me with many special memories. I was able to provide for my family while living out my dream of working with people in need. I wouldn't trade this time of my life for anything in the world.

In 1994, I became the Dean of Students for the Boys and Girls Choir Academy of Harlem. This is a prestigious school, and it's possible that is why the producers of *Glory Road* chose this as the "what they did in the future" fact during the closing montage scene of the movie. It is a performing arts school, made up of mostly inner city minority students who need to audition to be accepted. At the same time, there was a high priority put on academics and the student body consisted of many very well-rounded young people.

On a typical day, I would arrive early and oversee students coming in for breakfast. I'd walk the halls and make sure that students got to class on time. The halls were noisy, but a good kind of noisy. The students got along well and there was an overall positive vibe among them. These students wanted to be there and they wanted to stay out of trouble. There was an occasional fight here or there, or an accusation of theft, but overall there really weren't many hardcore discipline cases. If a student got in trouble, they were not allowed to perform and this was great leverage. These students were entertainers and in the same way athletes crave a field or court, they craved the stage. There were frequent talent shows and they were always amazing, Even though it was the 90's, the students did not perform hip-hop or modern music – which was fine by me since those styles are not my cup of tea. The choir director focused more on classical and spiritual music. The school broke students into two groups -- travel and local. The local group would, as the name implies, mostly perform around the New York City area. The travel group would make it outside of New York City, going around the world to perform for kings and queens -- and that is not an exaggeration.

About five years ago, I was contacted by a fifty-five year old grandfather named James Carwell. When he was younger, he was called "The Rabbit" because he was always bouncing around from place to place non-stop. He looked me up, and found out that I was the current varsity basketball coach at Spring Valley High School. He did some leg work and we reconnected. He was one of my students when I worked at Woodycrest. He called to thank me for all I did for him when I was Residential Director. He even put his daughter on the phone and she told me how much he talks about me and how much he credits me for steering him in the right direction. Ever since that first call, he has called me every Father's Day and also sent me a Father's Day card, thanking me for being the father figure he needed at the time. I cannot put into words how much that means to me. I dreamed of working in a profession that involved service to others, and a person in his fifties reached out to thank me for something that occurred decades earlier.

    Some people might look at my life and say that the 1966 N.C.A.A. Championship, or my Naismith Memorial Basketball Hall of Fame ring, proves that dreams do come true. I do believe that dreams come true, but for me, the proof is the Father's Day call and cards I get from James Carwell each year.

Chapter 14: The Mirror

"The tragedy of life doesn't lie in not reaching your goal. The tragedy lies in having no goal to reach. It isn't a calamity to die with dreams unfilled, but it is a calamity not to dream. It is not a disgrace to reach the stars, but it is a disgrace to have no stars to reach for. Not failure, but low aim, is a sin."

-Benjamin Mays

On Monday, March 3rd, 2014, I took a rare sick day from my job as a hall monitor at Spring Valley High School. I am the Head Coach of the Spring Valley High School varsity basketball team, and this was the day after our season ended. When I was in college, being run to death by Don Haskins, I was physically and emotionally drained when the season came to an end. Forty-eight years later, as a coach, I feel the same way when the season is over. This is how you should feel if you coach the right way. You need an edge to be a good coach. I want to win every game. Heck, I want to win every scrimmage. It doesn't matter to me. If someone is keeping score, I want to win. And even though I have never taken a shot or grabbed a rebound for Spring Valley, the season takes every ounce of my mind, body, and soul. And on this day, I was really feeling it. The funny thing is that when I was younger, I never in a million years would have thought I'd be a basketball coach. As much I loved the game, I never thought this was for me. I looked at it as a thankless job. Coaches are always second guessed and questioned. A part of me has "rabbit ears," and I didn't think I was thick skinned enough to handle the criticism. I guess I also pictured myself playing well into my nineties, winning a championship in a local senior citizen league that I'd start myself if I had to. On this morning, I went to the bathroom to shave and found myself staring into the mirror. It may have only been for ten or twenty seconds, but in that time, decades of coaching basketball flashed before my eyes.

I stumbled into coaching in 1982. Etta was playing C.Y.O. through St. Joe's school and church. At this point, because Roz was younger, she was a cheerleader for the team. Etta told her coach, Richard Durande, about my basketball background and he invited me to join the coaching staff, along with a man named Jim Reed. Richard and Jim would both become good friends of mine, and were both very dedicated individuals. The program is for young people from 4th through 8th grades, and Roz would eventually end up playing in the league as well. Coaching C.Y.O is a volunteer position; I wound up doing it for twenty years. Obviously, I was there long after Etta and Roz had outgrown it. Once I was exposed to coaching, I could never leave it. The only reason I ever left C.Y.O. was that working a full-time job and coaching there eventually became too much for me. If I had won the lottery, coaching C.Y.O. would have been my full-time job.

Coaching Roz was difficult, and I know Roz now has some of the same problems I did when she coaches my granddaughters, Kayla and Mahogany. If your child is not a good player, people want to know why he or she is on the court. If your child is skilled, like Roz, Kayla, and Mahogany, people will insist you are showing favoritism. With me and Roz, there were times I probably pushed her too hard. She was so good, and I so wanted her to utilize every ounce of her potential, that there were times when she would call my wife Claudia to come pick her up from games because she refused to ride in the car home with me. Other times, she'd get so mad that she wouldn't speak to me for a week. Richard Durande spoke to me about this and tried to help me ease up on her. I think at some point it almost became like Richard was Roz's coach and I was the coach of the rest of the team. C.Y.O. basketball is a state-wide program. When Roz was in 8th grade, we lost in the upstate championship and it was certainly a big letdown. However, I did have some very successful seasons. Coaching a boys' team, we won a 4th, 5th, 6th, 7th, and 8th grade championship. I don't care if it is basketball or a game of marbles, a championship is a championship and I am proud of this accomplishment. I didn't realize it at the time, but my success in C.Y.O. definitely helped my coaching career progress.

During the early 1980's, me and a bunch of other old-timers would get together for fun and play pick-up basketball games. By old-timers, I mean men in their 20's, 30's, and 40's. One of the players was Dr. Richard Greene, a New City, New York, resident and Superintendent of Schools for the Yorktown Heights School District. He got me an interview and I became an assistant on the boys' varsity basketball team there. I have a feeling that when the superintendent makes a call giving you a recommendation, your foot is certainly in the door. Yorktown was mostly a football and lacrosse school, but the basketball team was on the rise. My time there was invaluable. It gave me experience, and that experience helped me tremendously when I took on a new coaching job in 1983.

Spring Valley High School had a big year in 1982. The team won the state championship. Dave Sachs, an assistant coach on that team, moved over to Ramapo High School as their head coach. Ramapo High School is Spring Valley's sister school and biggest sports rival, even to this day. A junior varsity coach moved up to varsity assistant and I was hired as the Spring Valley junior varsity coach.

Lou Klewe was the Spring Valley varsity coach, Athletic Director, and the person who hired me in 1983. My coaching in C.Y.O. had gotten my name out in the community. Not only that, but some of the C.Y.O. players I coached from 4th through 8th grade were now entering high school. When Lou asked them about me, he got some nice reviews and decided to give me a shot. I really owe a lot to Lou. Besides hiring me, he did anything he could to help and advise me in my new position. A couple of years into my coaching tenure at Spring Valley, a budget crunch took away one of the basketball coaching positions. As the last one hired, I was the first to be let go. However, Lou let me stay on as a volunteer. I did this not only for my love of the game, but because all of my C.Y.O. players, who were in elementary school when I met them, were now the varsity squad. I looked at this as a project I needed to finish. As a volunteer, I went to every practice and game. I did this for about three or four years, and when a position opened back up again I'm sure my dedication to the program helped get me back on board. I was saddened to hear that Lou passed away a couple of years ago. He was a good friend and meant a lot to me.

    My transition from coaching C.Y.O. basketball, to junior varsity basketball for Spring Valley High School, was tougher than the one I made going from DeWitt Clinton to Texas Western. As a player, I always felt like I had control of the situation. As a coach, you have to trust someone else to carry things out for you. But in my early years of coaching, I learned what every high school and college coach in the country eventually comes to know. The X's and O's of coaching is one of the easiest parts of the job. It is also the smallest percentage of the job. Dealing with the human element of young people is the toughest part of the job. Teenagers deal with a lot of distractions that have nothing to do with basketball yet, in some ways, these things can easily come to have everything to do with basketball. For example, some people simply do not like to be told what to do. As someone who was nicknamed "Iron Head," I understand that. However, it doesn't mean I can coach effectively if players don't follow my instructions. Some players come to me never having been part of a team. Skills on a playground are a good foundation, but basketball, to me, is the ultimate team sport. You need to play as a team if you're going to win. Sometimes, I will encounter a young person who thinks they are much better than they are, and it can be earth shattering when they realize that they are not the next Michael Jordan or Lebron James. There is a transition period for a player to get a handle on their ability, and some players want success without putting in the hard work it takes to attain it. Parents all want their child to start. As a parent and grandparent of athletes, I completely understand that emotion, but, at the same time, everyone has to realize that there are only five starters on any basketball team. The majority of every team starts the game on the bench. Even just making the team has some parents thinking that colleges will be knocking on their door handing out scholarships. There are tens of thousands of high school coaches of every sport in this country, and can I guarantee you that every single one of them can relate to these issues. If you can find one that doesn't, please let me know. I'd love to know their secret.

And when I say all these things about the difficulties of coaching, please keep in mind, if it's not already obvious, how much I love it and how much it has enriched my life. I have already relayed my passion for human services and that is what coaching is. Being a coach is being a teacher, and the gym is my classroom. Like any coach, I've had some players who didn't care for me or my style. However, I can't tell you how many times I've had former players come back with their children to say hello and thank me. I've had former players thank me for making them men. I've had former players tell me that they wouldn't have made it as far in life as they did if it wasn't for my positive influence. I've even had some former players tell me that I was like a second father to them. Unfortunately, I found out that you cannot declare this on your tax return. All kidding aside, all of these things have meant so much to me. I have coached the sons of some of my players, and to me this is the ultimate sign of trust. They are willing to put their prize possessions under my supervision. Some of my former players have gone on to become coaches themselves. When I watch them on the sidelines -- and they look like a mini-me -- I feel so much pride. They thought enough of the way I coached to work it into their own style.

If you look at the four major professional sports -- baseball, football, hockey, and basketball -- I think you'll notice that a lot of the most successful coaches were not necessarily great players. For every Bill Russell or Joe Torre, who both had impressive playing and coaching careers, you see a coach who rode the bench or was a role player when they were competing. I think there are two reasons for this. First, a bench or role player spends a lot of time observing the game. This certainly comes in handy when strategy comes into play later on. Second, starting players have things come naturally to them. This is great as a player, but a coach needs to explain how and why to do things. A lot of starting players might not be able to communicate these concepts. I was a guard in high school and college. A guard, on some level, is the coach on the floor. My coaches told me the how's and why's that they did not always tell the other players. I know I'm biased, but I think this makes guards, in general, better coaches than centers. When I started at Spring Valley in the 1980s, I was in my forties and still a better athlete than my players. I had to adjust my style. I realized I couldn't assume that players knew how to do things that I could do. I had to demonstrate. I had to show them the how's and why's.

One of my favorite early demonstrations involved Roz. My players were struggling at the free throw line and I had access to a state champion free throw shooter -- my daughter. I invited Roz to practice as a guest lecturer, and she delivered. At first, the team of boys snickered about the idea of learning about sports from a girl. Then Roz hit ten free throws in a row. Snickers became questions. My 6'1" center at the time was the first to change his tune and embrace Roz's help. His name is Kevin Bullock. Kevin later went on to coach several sports at both Spring Valley and Ramapo High School. I should have known then that he'd become a great coach someday. He was open-minded and looking to improve his play to help the team. Years later, when Kevin got married, Roz and I attended the wedding.

As much as I was teaching in those early years, I was also getting on-the-job training and learning myself. I was able to get my players to focus on what was important. I had them concentrating on free throws over dunks, lay-ups over three pointers, and a "we" over a "me" philosophy. No team I have ever coached has had their name on the back of the jersey. I wanted one name on all of our jerseys -- Spring Valley. I implemented a coaching system that I call the Three A's: academics, attitude and athleticism. Academics mean you succeed in the classroom -- textbooks before playbooks. If you are academically ineligible, it's never going to matter how good of a player you are. Attitude means that you embrace the team concept, the key to successful basketball. And athleticism means you get your body and mind in shape to compete for the full thirty-two minutes of a high school basketball game.

As the years have gone by, and I have gained more and more experience as a coach, I have certainly noticed the similarities and differences I have with my two biggest coaching influences—Don Haskins and Hilton White. Coach Haskins taught me that you have to coach the complete person and that every player is different. What works for one player might not work for another. You have to know your players' strengths and weaknesses. You can't overwork your weaknesses and neglect your strengths. A player should never stop working on what he or she does best. Coach Haskins stressed conditioning, but it is different for me at the high school level. My players are younger and are not basketball lifers. I cannot expect the same things a coach would from a college player. I use conditioning as a way of teaching mental toughness. If you miss a free throw, the whole team runs. If you don't make three shots in a row, we all run for an extra ten minutes. I want to put some game pressure on the players so that when we play for real, they are prepared. Another thing I learned from Don Haskins was, of course, coaching defense. I certainly didn't learn offense from Coach Haskins. Moe Iba ran the offense at Texas Western. And as much as I love offense, and think that coaches who compete against me often think of me as an offensive-minded coach, I think Coach Haskins instilled in me a need to always put defense first.

That doesn't mean I don't love the offensive part of basketball, and that is where Hilton White's influence comes in. When Hilton White discovered me practicing basketball by myself, and took me under his wing, the first thing he did was teach me the right way to shoot a ball. Hilton and I were both from the parks and playgrounds of New York City, where offense was the attraction. Defense wins championships, but offense sure is fun. I love watching a game of run and gun basketball. Coach Haskins wanted us to pass the ball a thousand times before shooting, but defense in New York City involves scoring a lot and defending enough to win a high-scoring game; there was plenty of one-pass one-shot in New York. When Hilton coached me during summer league games, he had purpose behind his offensive plan. However, it was more like he'd give you the frame and let you paint your own picture. He gave us freedom to be ourselves and I try to do that as a coach. I think this is fun for the players and prepares them for any system that they might see if they play college basketball.

In the mid 1990's, Lou Klewe retired and Doug Carey took over as the Spring Valley varsity coach and I was named the junior varsity coach, which also meant that I'd work as an assistant for the varsity games. I mentioned that coaching is teaching, so Doug, as a social studies teacher at Spring Valley, came in with natural attributes that led to success on the court. Doug had coaching experience, and just as he is known for having patience with his history lessons, he was always very patient with developing our players. Like me, Doug knew that you have to coach the entire person. He'd learn about the players as people, ask them about their backgrounds, and figure out the best way to implement game plans. A leader is good at delegating authority, and Doug was willing to give me great input into what we were doing. We were on the same page as coaches, and to this day Doug is still someone I consider a great friend. In 1996, Spring Valley won the Golden Ball, which is the trophy given out to the Section One Champions. From a wins and losses standpoint, this was a highlight of my time working side-by-side with Doug.

In 1998, I took the job as the Spring Valley High School girls' varsity coach. Tony had been volunteering as an assistant with the junior varsity team, and he took the full-time position as J.V. coach. I took the girls' varsity job for two reasons. In a sense, it was a promotion and it was the first time I would be a varsity coach. More than that, I liked the idea of trying to take the girls' program to the next level. I could not pass up this new challenge. The Journal News, our local newspaper, ran a nice article about me taking the job. It was a bio piece and included some bullet point facts about me that you've already read about if you've made it to this point in the book. Doug Carey was interviewed for the article and he said: "I am pleased to know the man and not the legend. He wears many hats: dean, father, grandfather, and friend. He has been the foundation of our program and has been a tireless volunteer. He works on Sundays and all summer long. Legends don't do that. The man is as reliable as a rock." Doug saying those kind words meant so much to me, and if the Journal News ever interviews me about Doug it will be easy for me to return the compliment.

My first game as the girls' coach was a memorable one, although I think I am still trying to forget it. We were scheduled to play a school named R.C. Ketchum, and it was a road game. Our bus got lost on the way there, and we were an hour late. When we walked into the gym, the annoyed officials put twenty minutes up on the clock. The team had twenty minutes to change into their uniforms, warm up, and be ready for opening tip off. I think that if we weren't ready, the officials would have done jump ball and the R.C. Ketchum players would have stood under our basket unguarded firing shot after shot in our net like one of those basketball carnival games you see in arcades or at the Jersey Shore. We lost the game by forty-two points. It was demoralizing for me. I had never suffered a defeat like that before this game and I have never been a part of one after, thank goodness. I realized that I needed to tighten my belt, dig in, and keep working at doing what I knew best. We ended winning about half of our games that year, which actually wasn't too bad considering we only had one player on the team who was a senior. Most of the players had little basketball experience. The next year was a different story. We won about two thirds of our games. The team made it to the playoffs, but we lost in the sectional championship game. It was disappointing, but I knew the program was headed in the right direction.

In 2000, Doug Carey retired as the varsity coach and I was given the job that I still hold today. Spring Valley gave me the shot that I had been looking for, and to this day I am grateful. The funny thing is, the biggest worry I had when hired was having a repeat of the girls' R.C. Ketchum disaster. We won our first game of the season, and I think that really helped me relax and settle into the position. Being a high school coach is very different from coaching something like C.Y.O. Working in a high school, guiding young people towards smart choices, and helping them as good citizens, is more important than wins and losses. High school players represent a school out in the community and that is more important than hitting a free throw or hitting a lay-up. At this point, I was still working at the Boys and Girls Choir in Harlem, so I almost always had to race out of work to make it to Rockland in time for games and practices. This also forced me to rush to catch up with any news there was about my players -- checking in with student grades, making sure no one was facing discipline issues, etc. This is what led to the district hiring me full time as part of the security team at the school -- making me a hall monitor. By working in the building, I could keep an eye on my players and make sure they were succeeding in the classroom, the most important thing, so that they could succeed on the basketball court.

Through the years, in addition to coaching basketball, I have also helped coach track in the spring. Once someone is bitten by the coaching bug, it becomes a part of them forever. I always laugh when I hear people use the expression "brother from another mother," but I met mine in 2003 at a track meet. Syd McGready was a standout track star for Seton Hall College in the 1950's. He played basketball there as well. I was at a track meet and the athletic director from another school introduced us. Syd knew who I was, and asked if we could be introduced -- although our first conversation was brief, because Syd didn't want to bother me or take up too much of my time. Syd was a fixture at the local track meets so, over time, we started talking more and more until we became the best of friends. Syd's family is my family, and vice versa. I cannot say enough nice things about his lovely wife Judy, and the fact that his sons Steve and Anthony call me Uncle Willie certainly shows the bond we have. Soon after our friendship began, Syd joined the Spring Valley varsity coaching staff. I started him out with a salary of zero and, after eleven strong years, I gave him a raise to a salary of zero. Syd volunteers his time keeping stats during the game -- points, rebounds, assists, etc. I tease Syd that no one wants me to retire less than he does, because he has so much fun working with our players. He is such a special man.

Adam Vinatieri is an N.F.L. place kicker and has won four Super Bowl rings, three with the New England Patriots and one with the Indianapolis Colts. He was once asked which championship meant the most to him, and I loved his response. He said that he feels about the rings the way parents do about all of their children. He loves them all equally and each one is special in its own way. I think I feel the same way about all the teams I've coached through the years. Each team means so much to me. They have all been special for different reasons. The 2004-2005 squad, for example, holds a special place in my heart.

On December 21st, 2004, our team was 4-0. We wanted to keep our hot streak going and, to do so, we had to get past a team I had some history with. We got on the bus and headed down to the Bronx to face DeWitt Clinton -- my old school. Talk about life taking someone full circle. Forty years earlier, I did everything I could to help Clinton win basketball games, and now I had to do everything I could to make them lose. I couldn't help feeling nostalgic the entire day, as I had so many memories from my time there. We won the game 73-50. On January 15, 2005, I would have similar feelings when we again traveled to the Bronx, this time to play Samuel Gompers High School. Samuel Gompers High School was Dewitt Clinton's rival, and this is where Claudia's brothers, Donald and Gene, went to school. We won the game 68-60 and I was able to maintain my family bragging rights over my brothers-in-law into a second consecutive millennium. In addition to this game giving me a trip down memory lane, the win took our record to 13-0.

When we took the floor on February 18th, 2005, our record was 22-0. We were in the championship game against Mount Vernon, a powerhouse basketball school from Westchester -- a neighboring county of Rockland. Mount Vernon is always strong, with quality players on the court year-in and year-out. Ben Gordon, who graduated from Mount Vernon in 2000, and whom I coached against, is still in the N.B.A. as I write this book. This was a special opportunity for my players. I knew from a lifetime in the game that you never know when you will have a chance for a championship. This game was a big deal for me as well. I had won a championship as a high school player. I had won a championship as a college player. I had won championships with the C.Y.O., but I looked at a title as a varsity coach as the missing piece that would complete the puzzle of my basketball life. When the game against Mount Vernon was over, we walked away with our heads held high. We played our hearts out. We left everything we had out on the floor. But we also left without the championship, and I left without my final puzzle piece. Mount Vernon won the game 68-52.

That team was not special to me because of their undefeated regular season. It was much more than that. I had known all of the players since they were in 4th grade, as they had all played C.Y.O. for me. Seeing them grow from elementary school kids to young men meant a lot to me. They were one of the closest units I've ever coached. They all embraced the "We" mentality. They weren't necessarily the best group of players I had talent-wise, but they played the team game. And as good as they were on the court, they were even nicer off the court.

Weeks after the season ended, I was voted Coach of the Year at the County Awards Dinner. We participate in a very strong division and there are so many good coaches, so of course I was honored. We were 10-0 in the league that year, and to be honored and congratulated by coaches I competed against was special. But personal awards are not a priority for me; you are only as good as your last game, and we lost our last game. I would have gladly traded my award in for another chance at a title. I would have gladly traded it in for another crack at the powerhouse school, Mount Vernon.

I would get my wish during the 2013-2014 season. We entered the season with several good athletes on the team. Not only that, but some of our key players had been on the team for years, and experience is certainly an asset. However, we got off to a slow start. We were invited to play in a tournament called the Thomas Jefferson Showcase, and we did not fair well. Iona Prep had a 6'8" forward who was dominant. His teammates were happy to feed him the ball, and I think he took two thirds of their shots. But they played the team game. Iona players were not concerned about their own shots. They just wanted to win. Weeks later, we played in a tournament in Albany against a team called Catholic Central. The long ride up, sitting in traffic, did not help us play loose. In addition to that, one of our key players did not make the trip. We still gave it our all, but we lost 68-65. Over the Christmas break, we were invited to play in the prestigious Holiday Classic at the Westchester County Center. Again, we were pitted against Iona Prep, and again we came up short. But we were starting to get our game together.

On January 10th, we had a big game versus one of our main rivals in the conference, Clarkstown South. South has a very strong team and is well coached. We played very well. We brought our "A" game and won 75-65. It was Clarkstown South's only loss during the regular season. That was the good news for us. The bad news was that, after a string of victories, we played South again with different results. It was the final game of the season, and South beat us 72-70. For me, this was the most disappointing loss of the season. It was a back and forth game, but one that we could have had if we played our best. But we didn't play together as a team. The loss had immediate consequences. We dropped into a tie for the league championship and were given a #6 seed for the playoffs. Clarkstown South helped their cause with this win and was the #2 seed.

On February 20th, 2014, we traveled across the Tappan Zee Bridge to play the #3 seed, White Plains High School. It was the Section 1, Class AA quarterfinals. I knew we were up for a big challenge. Road games are tough on any level of competition. Similarly to how our season began, we got off to a slow start. At some point, we were trailing by double digits. But our players refused to quit. We chipped away and chipped away at the lead. When the final buzzer sounded, we squeaked out a 69-66 victory. I was very proud of the players.

On February 27th, it was time for the rubber match against Clarkstown South. We both had big victories against each other during the regular season, and now a trip to the conference finals was on the line. We were so far along in the playoffs at this point that this was a neutral site game. It was held at the Westchester County Center, which has a capacity of close to 4,000 people for a basketball game. Next year, the New York Knicks will be using this arena for their D league team. For players in high school, this is a big time game. We showed up. Unlike the White Plains game, we got off to a good start and built up a lead. But Clarkstown South would not quit. They kept on passing, shooting, and competing hard. They chipped away at our lead, but we held them off. The final score was 67-66. We made it to the finals and it was one of our best efforts of the year. Our chemistry was there and that put us over the top. Three of our four starters had four fouls, so eleven of our thirteen players played. It was a real team win.

Success for a varsity team goes way beyond just the coach and players. It really takes so many people working together to have success. My athletic director, Bill Pilla, has been such a great asset for me through the years. Having an A.D. who has your back is a great feeling. Bill is a coach himself, so he knows what I go through. He has great insight. And even though I have been talking to the media since I was a teenager, it is still not necessarily my specialty. Bill will sometimes take care of this for me so I can have time to get my players ready before a game. Bill goes out of his way to give me and his other coaches what we need. Howard Arciniegas is the school athletic trainer. He is amazing. He is not only an expert of the body, but of the mind. He can fix players up when they are hurt, but he also knows when a player has a nagging injury that might be related to not wanting to go to practice. There is no way our sports program would be the same without his tireless efforts.

My family and I run a charity event each year called the Willie Worsley shootout. Teams from the tri-state area come to our school to play against each other. It is a lot of fun, as well as a ton of work, in particular, for Roz and Tony. Joel Klein, the Superintendent of the East Ramapo School District, has gone out of his way to tell me that he would do anything he could to help us continue this tournament. For someone as busy as he is to reach out to me like that shows the support system I have at Spring Valley. In the days leading up to the Mount Vernon game, all of our school administrators -- Principal Karen Pinel, Assistant Principals Fran Petersel, Dionne Olamiju, and Paul Finklestein all made a point of stopping by to see me and give me encouraging words. They were all in attendance when we hit the floor of Westchester County Center for the game against Mount Vernon. And when I won my 200th career game as a varsity coach during the season, the administrators spread word around the building and made P.A. announcements of congratulations. Paul Finklestein and I have an amazing DeWitt Clinton coincidence/connection. His fraternal twin brother is the current DeWitt Clinton head basketball coach. In 2013, Paul and his brother presented me with a DeWitt Clinton Varsity basketball jacket to commemorate the 50th anniversary of my 1963 high school championship and M.V.P. game. This gift is one of my prized possessions and when I went to hug Paul, I was overcome with emotion and he jokingly asked me to be careful not to get his shirt wet with my tears of appreciation.

Greg Downey is the Head of Security at Spring Valley. He does such an amazing job with the students of our school, both inside and outside of the building. Besides organizing the security for sporting events, Greg, a huge Knicks fan, organizes fan buses for road games. This was a big road game and the Tigers of Spring Valley wanted to be there. By the time the refs threw the ball up for opening tip off, hundreds of Spring Valley students, as well as teachers, were in the stands cheering us on. Tiny Archibald and Ernie Brown, a former Rucker Park teammate of mine, came to the game as well to support me. I was very excited. When we lost to Mount Vernon in 2005, I immediately wished for another crack at them. All I had to do was wait around 3,300 days and my wish came true. I got my chance on March 2, 2014.

It was a very quiet, quiet bus ride on the way home from the Westchester County Center. As we sat in traffic on the Tappan Zee Bridge, crossing the Hudson River felt like it was taking as long as it would to swim across the ocean. As Tiny said to me after the game, "If you don't put the ball in the basket, you don't win." He kept it short and sweet, but it was right on the money. We lost 47-39. If I was to give a scouting report on the game, I'd say that we had the athletic edge, but they played with better chemistry, and whipping up that chemistry is my responsibility as the coach. In the locker room after the game, I didn't give a long speech. That is not my style. I thanked the team for putting up with me all season and I apologized for not getting them a championship. They are young people still trying to grow, and I am their coach. I learned from Coach Haskins that protecting your players is a lifetime obligation. And, as is the curse of coaching, of course I couldn't help but second guess myself. Did I do everything I could to prepare us to win? Were we all too excited about the opportunity? Could I have done something to offset the high emotions we were all feeling? And the more people came up to me offering support right after the loss, the worse I felt.

I have been chasing after Mount Vernon like a dog endlessly chasing his own tail, but I don't think I have another 3,300 days of coaching in me to catch them. I do have next year, though. And if I never win a championship as a varsity coach, it will not be a failure. It would only be a failure if I stopped trying to win a championship.

On Monday, March 3rd, 2014, I took a rare sick day from my job as a hall monitor at Spring Valley High School... On this morning, I went into the bathroom to shave and found myself staring into the mirror. It may have only been for ten or twenty seconds, but in that time, decades of coaching basketball flashed before my eyes.

Chapter 15: My Girl

"When someone you love dies, and you're not expecting it, you don't lose her all at once; you lose her in pieces over a long time—the way the mail stops coming...Gradually, you accumulate the parts of her that are gone. Just when the day comes—when there's a particular missing part that overwhelms you with the feeling that she's gone, forever—there comes another day, and another specifically missing part."
John Irving, *A Prayer for Owen Meany*

Intertwined with all the stories I've told you so far about my life in human services and my work as a basketball coach, my family, like all families, was touched by the circle of life—birth and death—death and birth. This planet relies on these elements coexisting, and I'm not sure which one makes you sit back more and realize how precious every day of life is.

By the mid 1990's, my mother, Julia, was living in Brooklyn with her Aunt Rosalie. Rosalie was more like a mother than an aunt to my mother, and as my mother got increasingly sick, Rosalie did an amazing job as her caregiver. My mother, a heavy smoker, was diagnosed with throat cancer. My mother's already petite frame was slowly withering away.

While my mother was living with Rosalie, and Etta and Roz were getting older, it became harder to go see her. We talked on the phone constantly, but I did not visit her enough. This is something that still pulls at my heart. Claudia and I were so busy with work and raising kids that a phone call was more convenient than traveling from our one bedroom basement apartment in The Bronx to Brooklyn. I consider this a reason we didn't visit enough, but not a good excuse.

When my mother was in the hospital, with very little time left, we did not take the girls to see her. Julia had lost so much weight that we felt Etta and Roz might be frightened to see her. We didn't want that to be the last image they had of their grandmother -- gaunt, frail, and with a million wires and tubes sticking out of her body. During one of my last hospital visits, a nurse told me what an amazing woman my mother was. My mother never complained to anyone in the hospital about all the pain she was in; complaining was just not in her stoic nature. Harry Belafonte had a famous song, "Man Smart, Woman Smarter.' I agree with that and I think he could have had a follow up hit with, "Man Strong, Woman Stronger." When it comes to being sick, men are wimps. Because I always admired my mother so much, I have tried to follow her lead and be strong when I don't feel well. I don't complain, but sometimes this will drive my family crazy. I once had a bad case of gout and the pain was unbearable. I didn't even tell my daughters and when they found out, they were furious that I had kept it from them. For me, if my mother could face throat cancer with such courage, what could I have that would justify complaints? When I don't feel well, I like to be left alone and deal with it myself.

My mother's death taught me a valuable life lesson. You never know when someone you love is going to leave you, so I make a point of always telling people I love them. I was never going to make the mistake I felt I did with my mother, by not being there enough or telling her I loved her enough.

My mother had two services, one in Brooklyn, and one down South. She was buried in Virginia Beach, which is close to our original home of Norfolk, Virginia. It was during the service in Virginia Beach that her death really hit home, and I finally processed all the feelings I had. I knew how much pain she was in so, on some level, the idea of her resting in peace gave me some peace of mind. But a part of me also felt selfish. I couldn't bear to see her leave me and I wanted her back. I lost two friends with one death -- my best friend and my first friend. During my childhood, it was me and her against the world. She was the greatest, and I could not love or idolize someone more as a person, parent, and friend. Julia Worsley was an amazing woman!

Ten years after my mother passed away, my father, Orange Buck, joined her in heaven. Earlier in the book, I mentioned the phone call I received at work telling me the news. The call came from my cousin Ellen. The funny thing is that I never knew my cousin Ellen. She knew who I was though, and had been following my career in the newspapers, from my playing days all the way through my coaching career. I'm glad she called. Love is not like a light switch that can be easily turned on and off. Even though a lot of time had passed since I saw my father, I always loved him. I needed to grieve this loss.

Claudia and I headed down South for the services. When Claudia and I checked into our hotel, we met a Worsley working here and a Worsley working there. A big part of that trip was meeting people from both sides of my family whom I never knew before. I spent time with my step brother, William Earl Spain and my step sister, Samantha Buck. She was the only one out of all of us who took my father's last name. Samantha was younger than Etta, and we all laughed about the fact that Etta was older than her own aunt.

A couple of years ago, I got a terrible call from William Earl telling me that Samantha had passed away. In general, I do not deal well with death and this one hurt for several different reasons. Not only did I grieve because my sister, someone so young, was dead, but I also grieved for all the time that had gone by without us connecting, and then, shortly after we finally did, she was taken from me.

When Etta first started to date, I didn't want to know anything about it. I'm sure I'm not the only father to struggle with going from the only man in his daughter's life to the second man in his daughter's life. I struggled with the idea, but Claudia helped me to get over it, pointing out the successful relationship we had at such a young age.

Etta married her husband Greg when she was in her mid-twenties. Roz was her maid of honor and one of my favorite pictures is of the two of them on this special day, both looking radiant. I was oblivious to a lot of the wedding traditions, and I found out a couple of days before the wedding that I had to pick a song for me and Etta to dance to. After some soul searching, I chose "My Girl" by The Temptations.

> I've got sunshine on a cloudy day.
> When it's cold outside I've got the month of May.
> I guess you'd say
> What can make me feel this way?
> My Girl (my girl, my girl)
> Talkin' bout my girl (my girl)

There was only one thing about the wedding that kept from making it the perfect day. Etta wore heels and, when we hit the dance floor, she was taller than I was.

Etta and Greg moved to Patterson, New Jersey and then to Pennsylvania. But the geographical distance didn't create any distance between us. She would call me several times a week, even if she only had a minute or two to spare, to see how I was. She was always checking to see that I was taking my medicine and doing the things I was supposed to do to be healthy. Etta was born to be a great mother.

Etta and Greg's first child, my first grandchild, was a boy. He is named David and when I first saw him I thought he looked like a dark skinned version of me. The doctor's said he was going to be tall, and I have to admit that I wondered if he might turn into the next Willie Worsley on the basketball court. However, Greg was more of a baseball fan and I think David gravitated in that direction in his early years of playing sports. He and I would have fun shooting the basketball around when I'd visit, but eventually sports faded from the picture. David is very smart and his success came in the classroom. He is now in college and I am so proud of the person he is.

Etta and Greg's second child was a girl. Her name is Nicole and she is beautiful. As she got older, we all realized that she was the spitting image of Greg's sister. Tall and thin, I think she gave basketball a try, but ultimately ended up gravitating towards music and applying her talents in the school marching band. Nicole also does a great job in the classroom and she will be graduating high school this year.

Etta and Greg had a third child named Michael. I pushed Etta to have him named Willie after me, but she compromised and gave him the middle name James, which is my middle name. When Michael was young, I noticed that he had a tough time talking and communicating. My family knows that I have a hard time dealing with serious issues, and Etta tried for as long as she could to shield me from the news. Michael was born having some special needs. Michael understands you when you talk to him, but he struggles with speech. He has learned sign language to help, and people who are around him a lot know what he is trying to say just fine. David, as the older brother, has become a bodyguard for Michael and I think it is so sweet how he and Nicole protect him. There is a frustration for me that I am not able to communicate with Michael the way I would love to. I don't see him as much as the rest of my family does, so I have the toughest time of all conversing with him. Michael is a big teddy bear and I love him very much.

Roz followed Etta's blueprint when it came to dating and kept me in the dark. As a teenager, we'd go shopping together at the mall and she'd make me walk way ahead of her. I quickly realized this was so she could talk to boys if she wanted to without me cramping her style. When Roz was in her twenties, she and Tony started to give me more wonderful grandchildren.

Brianana was born in between Nicole and Michael. As a child, Brianana looked like Roz but, as she gets older, I think she looks more like Tony. Brianana reminded us all so much of Etta that we actually started to call her "Little Etta." She was always sweetly nosy and curious and had a good question for every topic under the sun. Some kids have the terrible twos, but I think Brianana had the terrible twos, threes, fours and beyond. I say that jokingly and only to point out what a great personality Brianana has.

Four years after Brianana was born, Roz and Tony gave me two more grandchildren: twin girls named Mahogany and Kayla. Mahogany is one minute older than Kayla and, like most twins, she won't let Kayla forget that fact. When they were young, I was able to tell them apart by their cheeks. Mahogany had skinny little cheeks and Kayla had adorable chubby cheeks. It's funny for me now to see the different personalities they have, even though they are twins. Mahogany is quiet and reserved like me, while Kayla can talk a mile-a-minute without breaking a sweat. They are both gym rats and great athletes. Even though they were the last grandchildren that I was blessed with, they are the most likely to carry on the Worsley name on the basketball court.

When Etta and Roz were little, they'd love to play school together. Roz would play the dutiful student, while Etta would come home and teach her everything she learned that day from her teachers. In addition to Claudia's natural smarts, I think this is why I have such smart grandchildren. Etta and Roz learned so much from each other at a young age and that knowledge has been passed down to the next generation. What I wouldn't do to watch them play one more game of school as little girls.

December 6th, 2010 was the worst day of my life. The Spring Valley Basketball team was headed to Newark, New Jersey for a scrimmage when Tony received a phone call. Tony calls me "Doc" and I will never forget the look on his face as he said "Doc, we have to turn the bus around." He was trying to be calm, but I knew something was very wrong. I called the coach of the opposing team and explained that I had a family emergency. I didn't know any details yet, but I knew it was a family emergency.

As we drove back to Spring Valley, I carefully observed Tony. I could see he was devastated, but not "parent" devastated. I knew it wasn't Roz, Brianana, Mahogany, or Kayla that I needed to be worried about. When my athletes were dismissed and the bus drove away, Tony and I jumped in his car and headed towards Pennsylvania. And that's when I heard the news that has changed my life forever.

Roz got a frantic phone call and raced over to Etta's house. When Roz got there, Etta was sprawled out on the kitchen floor. She was dead. When Tony told me this story, I broke down and wailed over and over again, "Why not me? Why not me?" And although my mouth has stopped saying these words, my heart never has. It should have been me. I know I am not the first person to ever say this, but no parent should know the pain of outliving their child. My beautiful daughter was gone, and I was not expecting it.

I have decided to maintain some privacy for my family and not get too much into the details of Etta's passing, other than to say that she died of natural causes. Ultimately, what killed my daughter is not important. Whatever took her is not giving her back to me, and that is the greatest tragedy of my life.

The next few days were a blur. When I am upset, I need to be by myself and I sat a few rows away from my family at the wake in the funeral home. I was still in a state of shock. Claudia came up to me, put her hand on mine, and simply said, "I know Will. I know." What could be said at that moment to make either of us feel better?

The final service took place in an old fashioned sermon hall. Etta worked in her local school district and the place saw many mourners stop by to pay their respects. My longtime friend John Boykin and friend and coworker Sue McGill came all the way from New York to be there. They didn't even know Etta, and that fact really made their trip touching to me. I'm sure other friends from New York made the trip, but my memory of the day is still foggy. When we went back to Etta's house after the service, I could see how drained everybody was. We all tried our best to deal with it, but each of us was suffering. Kayla and her Aunt Etta were very close. Even now, Kayla will call me up crying just to talk about Etta. She and I have certainly leaned on each other a lot for support.

Etta died on December 6th. Her birthday is December 16th. My birthday is December 13th. Claudia's birthday is December 20th and Roz's birthday is January 8th. From the time Roz was born, and our family was complete,

December and January was not just Christmastime -- it was a time to celebrate all of us. Our birthdays all basically fell within the same month. Now, December is a month I dread. I know the holidays are tough for a lot of people who have lost someone they love, and I have now joined that unfortunate group. The holidays take a physical and emotional toll on me and I don't ever see that getting better. I think if I could hibernate like a bear and wake up sometime after the holidays, I would do it in a second. I think of Etta every day, and with every breath that I take.

Well, I guess you'd say
What can make me feel this way?
My Girl
My Girl
My Girl
Talkin' bout My Girl.

My Girl

Chapter 16: Glory Road

This is it
It all begins here
My stomach bundles up in fear
Walked in, to hear the crowd the boo
But playing ball is all we do
Even though we really tried
Still no one is on our side
It's the last game, of the year
Champions is the only word
We hear
I know my teammates have my back
Time to take the ball
To the rack
U.T.E.P. Doesn't Rest!
Until they all know who is the best
From all of us
To all of you
Number one is the best we can do!
             -Brianana Wooten

    This poem was written by my beautiful granddaughter Brianana. Who would have known when she wrote it that I'd be using it to open a chapter in my autobiography that details a Hollywood movie made about an amazing time of my life? "From all of us to all of you, number one is the best we can do," was said by Willie Cager to the El Paso community when our plane landed following the 1966 Championship win against Kentucky. I love how Brianana wove those words into her poem, but more than that I love her and the fact that she wrote this for me!

    Don Haskins was originally approached with the idea of making a movie about the 1966 N.C.A.A. Championship, which eventually became the movie *Glory Road*. At first, he did not like the idea. Most people would jump at the chance to have a movie made about their life. He didn't. And the funny thing is, the reason he didn't like the idea was because originally the story was going to be all about him. The first premise for the movie was one that would be all about Don Haskins and his coaching career. It would chronicle all he went through and I'm sure it would have highlighted the death threats he faced. But, as I mentioned earlier, Don Haskins looked at coaching as a lifetime job, and, once again, he protected his players. He agreed to go along with the movie, and from what I understand it was grudgingly, knowing it would probably happen with or without him, only if the roles of his players were part of the story. Coach Haskins could have taken all the money that a Hollywood studio was willing to pay for the story and kept it all for himself, but he didn't. He made sure that everyone, from the players, to the other coaches, to the trainers, was given their fair share. Maybe this is why my favorite part of the movie is his cameo. He plays a gas station attendant and you can see him filling up someone's car. Every time I see that scene I smile and take a second to think of what a special person he was.

Steve Tredennick was a couple of years older than me and also played guard, before my time, for Coach Haskins and the Texas Western Miners. Like almost all of Coach Haskins' former players, he felt a great loyalty for the man. Steve was a lawyer and took on the task of seeing Don Haskins' vision of the movie happen. He reached out to the players from the team for permission to use their stories so that the movie project could proceed. Harry Flournoy, our team captain, was one of the first people contacted and he and Steve were the ones who really kept me in the loop about what was going on. I don't have an email address and I never will. In fact, I would have an easier time contacting someone with drum beats or smoke signals than using my computer. Needless to say, Steve and Harry called me on the phone a lot. Steve eventually became the lawyer for the players on the team as well.

All of the players from the team, black and white, were compensated for the portrayal of their lives on screen. As I wrote earlier, we were not two different groups made up by race. We were one team. We were one team when we won the 1966 Championship game, and we were one team when the movie version of *Glory Road* was in the early stages of development. We were united and still had each other's backs. The wheels were set in motion and the movie started to happen.

Glory Road eventually became a Walt Disney production. That was certainly a selling point for me. It would be a family movie. The idea was for the movie to touch people of all races and ages. I think that was best way to approach the project.

The process of casting the movie began. The studio used old pictures of the players and started auditions. One day, I got a phone call from an actor named Sam Jones III. He was cast to play the most handsome member of our team, Willie Worsley. He called me "Mr. Worsley" and I think that he was nervous about picking my brain for the role. I tried to use humor to make him feel at ease with me. I told him that I hoped he was shorter than me, and that he better work hard because I am better looking than he is. Sam asked me a lot of basketball questions. How did I prepare for games? What were my favorite moves? Could I dunk? I think he also wanted to hear my accent so he could work that into his performance. He even asked me about facial expressions. He must have heard that I was nicknamed "Iron Head." I think his main concern was approaching the basketball/athletic element of the role.

I know I might sound biased, but I think Sam Jones III had the most similar likeness to his real-life counterpart of all the actors portraying team members. And when I finally met Sam Jones III, I felt really good about him as a person. He was such a nice young man. He always treated me with respect, like he was talking to a legend. The funny thing is, his grandfather is an absolute basketball legend. Sam Jones was a ten time N.B.A champion with the Boston Celtics. His number was retired by the team and like my oldest friend, Nate "Tiny" Archibald, he is a member of the N.B.A. 50th anniversary team.

The studio arranged a meet and greet for the players and actors in El Paso. Many scenes in the movie were shot on location in El Paso, as well as New Orleans. Tim Floyd was one of the first people I ran into upon arriving. For nine years, Tim served as an assistant for Coach Haskins. In the late 1990's, Tim took over coaching the Chicago Bulls after Michael Jordan and Phil Jackson left the team. He is currently the head coach at U.T.E.P. Tim was hired as the Basketball Consultant for the movie. I think he was a great choice. He knows Don Haskins, knows the community and people of El Paso, and he certainly knows basketball. Tim has always been very supportive of our 1966 Championship team and I've always appreciated that.

Josh Lucas, who starred in movies like *Sweet Home Alabama*, *The Hulk*, and *A Beautiful Mind*, was cast as Don Haskins. Emily Deschanel, who was the female lead on the television show *Bones* was cast as Don's wife, Mary Haskins. They were both so genuine and nice. They treated the players like we were the Hollywood stars and each of them called me Mr. Worsley. Eventually, after we had met several times, they finally called me Willie and I actually felt relieved. They finally felt friendly enough with me to call me by my first name.

Jerry Bruckheimer, and his movie company, in association with Walt Disney Pictures, produced the movie. In addition to *Glory Road*, he has produced some other movies that I heard have done well: *Top Gun*, *The Pirates of the Caribbean*, *Beverly Hills Cop*, *Pearl Harbor*, *Crimson Tide*, *Remember the Titans* and *Gone in 60 Seconds*. As you can see, I only work with the top producers in the business. But seriously, for such a successful person, Jerry was very down-to-earth and easy to talk to. He took the time to explain his vision for the film. Initially, I was disappointed because I thought *Glory Road* would be more of a basketball movie. But Jerry, and the director, James Gartner, as well, explained that basketball was the hook -- a vehicle to show what was happening in the 1960's. There are a lot of sports movies that get made. However, *Glory Road* was going to be a sports history movie. After Jerry laid it out for me, I knew he was right. This movie could both entertain and educate people about a hugely important time in American history.

Bobby Joe Hill and David Lattin were the stars of our team so, logically, their characters were going to be the players featured the most in the film. I think that Jerry Bruckheimer felt that the New York City connection of Nevil Shed, Willie Cager, and me had strong potential in the story arc. They were looking for me to have an outstanding characteristic. In *Glory Road*, Nevil's character was used to show the tough, no-nonsense approach of Don Haskins. Willie Cager had a heart murmur in real life, and that was his character's focus in the movie. Then there was me. Being the shortest member of the team wasn't enough of a storyline, so they took the angle of making me militant. There is a scene in the movie where I have a Black Power poster above my dorm room bed. The movie is "based" on a true story and if you've read the book to this point, hopefully you know that I am not a militant person. I have had white friends all my life and have never really considered myself a political person. However, there were many people living in The Bronx in the 1960's who did hold these views. Would I have liked it better if they made my character the one who scored all the points? – maybe, but I always felt like Jerry Bruckheimer really liked me and this was a way for my character to have more lines in the film. Several of the players on the team stayed in El Paso for a bit to watch some of the scenes getting shot. I wasn't able to do so. I returned to New York to coach my team.

    I have to admit that the first two times I watched *Glory Road*, I mostly focused in on my character. I was curious how they had portrayed me. How many lines did I have? How many scenes was I in? I think it wasn't until the third time seeing the movie that I went from liking it, to loving it. I saw the "big picture" and I think Jerry succeeded in his vision to use basketball as a way of teaching history. People ask me all the time how I feel about the movie and I truthfully think it is wonderful. In 2016, it will be fifty years since we won our big game against Kentucky. The movie has kept our names out there and introduced a whole new generation of people to our story.

    The first premiere of the movie took place in El Paso and, as I told you, I watched it hand-in-hand with my "airplane mother," who years earlier helped me survive my plane ride from New York to Texas. The second premiere took place at the Pantages Theatre, 6233 Hollywood Boulevard, Hollywood, California. By including the full address, I get to mention twice that I was in Hollywood. How did I end up at a Hollywood movie premiere? One of my favorite parts of the night was that the studio gave me a limousine, all to myself, to pull up to the Red Carpet. I was still scarred by having to always sit in the middle, back seat of cars during my early years, so spreading out in a huge car felt great. When I walked down the Red Carpet into the theatre, I tried to look cool, calm, and collected. I put on my "Bronx" face to give off the vibe that I was unaffected by the glamour of the event. In reality, my knees were shaking from nervousness. Don Haskins was not able to travel to the premiere, as his health was in decline. However, he would have been proud of me that night. He always wanted his team to have sweaty hands before the big games, and my hands were plenty sweaty that night.

Academy Award winner Jon Voight played Adolph Rupp and was at the premiere. So was Pat Riley, and other Los Angeles sports stars like A.C. Green and Eric Dickerson. Alicia Keys, whose vocals are featured throughout the movie, was there as well. And here I was being photographed alongside these famous people. The inside of the Pantages Theatre was beautiful. It is one of those old school Hollywood movie palaces and it reminded me of Radio City Music Hall in New York. When the movie was finished, the crowd reaction was what we were hoping for. The movie eventually got good reviews and spent several weeks as the number one movie in the country.

On January 13th, 2006, *Glory Road* opened nationwide. The studio arranged for me Josh Lucas, and Derek Luke, who played Bobby Joe Hill, to attend a Knicks game as a way of promoting the movie. We had courtside seats. Famed movie director and die hard Knicks fan Spike Lee, who was sitting one row in front of us, came over to me and said, "It's about time they did you guys justice." That really meant a lot to me. I know Spike loves sports, but you can also tell through his movies that he has a real appreciation of history and the role race has played in this country. Greg Downey, my friend from Spring Valley is also a die hard Knicks fan and has season tickets. His seats are not as good as Spike Lee's. Greg was able to convince security that I was his uncle, and he came down and took some pictures with us. When they showed the *Glory Road* crew up on the big screen, we got a great reaction from the crowd and it felt really nice. Forty-three years after winning a high school championship for Dewitt Clinton High School, I was back at Madison Square Garden promoting a movie about another chapter in my basketball life. It was hard to believe.

Living in the northeast, and being the coach at Spring Valley High school, made me an easy person for the media to get in contact with. Several local papers got in touch with me to ask about *Glory Road*. The questions were usually some variation of "How did you feel to be portrayed in a movie?" My answer was always something like, "I wish I was in better shape so I could have played myself." Answering questions to the media about the movie did not feel special to me, but the reaction of the students at Spring Valley High School was very fun. Most of them might not have even realized I was being portrayed in the movie. However, during the closing credits of *Glory Road*, the real life me, David Lattin, and Pat Riley talk about the game. This helped people match the name to the face. Some students and staff would ask to take pictures with me. Some students felt shy about asking me. I had a student walk by me several times, looking me up and down, before finally asking, "Are you the one in that movie?" My favorite question was when a student said, "Why are you here, aren't you a movie star?" I know I have movie star good looks, but I still had to correct him. It was heartwarming to see that. And as much as it was a special time in my life, the movie also made for a special time for the entire Spring Valley High School community.

In early February of 2006, I received the most surprising piece of mail I have ever gotten. It was addressed to me at home, and the return address said -- The White House.
Inside the envelope was an invitation that read:

> **The President and Mrs. Bush**
> **Request the pleasure of your company**
> **At a dinner to be held at**
> **The White House**
> **On Wednesday, February 22, 2006**
> **At six-thirty o'clock**
> **East Entrance**

The 1966 N.C.A.A. Championship Basketball Team, the Texas Western Miners, was invited for a before-dinner screening of *Glory Road*. When I was a little boy, my mother and I lived in a small apartment with an outhouse for a bathroom. If someone had told me then that I'd even be invited to anyone's house for dinner someday, I probably wouldn't have believed it. I didn't expect to ever know someone who owned a house. Now I was being invited to The White House. The White House symbolizes America, and I think my teammates and I symbolize the American Dream. When we won the N.C.A.A. Championship in 1966, Texan Lyndon Johnson was president. Johnson signed the Civil Rights act into law in 1964. But when the Texas Western Miners from El Paso defeated Kentucky, we were not invited to The White House to visit, which is a tradition in American sports. I wonder if we are the only team to ever win a championship and be invited to The White House forty years later to celebrate.

President George W. Bush was also from Texas and a huge sports fan. He and The First Lady, Laura Bush could not have been nicer to us. They asked us questions, laughed, joked, and really made us all feel at home. Because they made us feel so relaxed, I did not have the sweaty palms that I did at the movie premiere. It's funny to think that I was more nervous in front of entertainment photographers than I was talking to the leader of the free world. We presented the Bush family with some signed gifts and we took a ton of pictures. Weeks later, I got a thank you note from President Bush for the gifts. The note also complimented *Glory Road* and said, "I appreciate your commitment to greatness and your historic achievement." A signed note from the President of the United States makes for quite a souvenir.

On April 1, 2006, we all traveled to Indianapolis for the N.C.A.A. Final Four. During halftime of the finals between Florida and George Mason, a game eventually won by Florida, the 1966 Texas Western team, with Tina Hill representing Bobby Joe, just as she had done at The White House, was introduced to the crowd. It was a special moment for us all, as we were being honored on the 40th anniversary of our win over Kentucky. It really showed how much things had changed in America. When we won in 1966, we weren't even given a ladder to take down the net. Now, we got a standing ovation from the crowd. I could feel the goose bumps on my arms.

On July 16th, 2006, I found myself back in Los Angeles for the second time that year. ESPN has an annual event called The ESPYS, which is almost like the Academy Awards for the sports world. Just like the *Glory Road* premiere, it was a Red Carpet event. I felt more comfortable this time. Maybe it was because by then, I had been to a Red Carpet event before. Maybe it was because, instead of actors, I was surrounded by athletes, which is definitely more in my comfort zone. The whole team made the trip, as *Glory Road* was nominated for Best Sports Movie of the Year. We won. Don Haskins was too ill to travel to the event, so his wife, Mary, represented him and accepted the award on behalf of the team. It was yet another special, magical night for me and my teammates.

2006 was a whirlwind year for me. In between working my job, walking the halls of Spring Valley High School, and coaching the varsity team, I was attending Red Carpet events in Hollywood, getting honored at the N.C.A.A. Final Four, and attending dinner at the White House with the President and First Lady of the United States. And as unbelievable as that all was, 2007 turned out to be just as amazing. The Naismith Memorial Basketball Hall of Fame received an application nominating our team for enshrinement. Our *Glory Road* was just beginning.

Chapter 17: The Hall

"Be Strong in Body, clean in mind, lofty in ideals."
James Naismith

In late 2005, I got a call from our team lawyer Steve Tredennick. They were probably done shooting the movie and were in the post-production phase of editing for the early 2006 release of the film. He told me that there was talk, by the General Mills Company, of putting a picture of our team on a box of Wheaties I played it cool when I talked on the phone with Steve, but inside this news got my blood pumping. Younger people reading this book might not appreciate what it means for an athlete to be on a box of Wheaties. The Wheaties cover has always been a symbol of greatness in the world of athletics. Muhammad Ali, when he was heavyweight champ, Bruce Jenner, when he won the gold in the decathlon in the 1976 Olympics, Walter Payton, the Hall of Fame running back -- these were the types of people who were on a box of Wheaties. As much as I was excited, I refused to believe this was going to happen. I didn't want to set myself up for a let down.

About two weeks after Steve called, I got a package in the mail. It had a small Wheaties box, the size of a postcard, with our picture on it. Not only that, it was my picture taking down the net after the Texas Western win over Kentucky in 1966. I was floored. I thought they were going to use the famous team photo of all of us with the trophy when we returned to El Paso. Instead, I was on the front with pictures of Coach Haskins, David Lattin, Willie Cager and Bobby Joe on the back. It was really happening.

Michael Jordan has set the record for the number of times on the cover of a box of Wheaties. He has been on eighteen times. Now I'm not comparing myself to Michael Jordan. Who could? But I did have a fun fantasy run through my mind after getting the Wheaties postcard and the news it was a done deal. Play along with me for a minute. Michael Jordan and I happen to get on the same elevator together. A stranger comes running to jump in and just makes it before the doors close. After the person catches their breath, they say, "Hey, haven't I seen you on a box of Wheaties?" At the same time, Michael and I both say "Yes!" Now wouldn't that make a great commercial?

On November 29th, 2005, the team members once again gathered in El Paso for the debut of the Wheaties box. 6,000 fans showed up in the gym to cheer us on. Nevil Shed, who put me on his shoulders when that picture was taken, and I went out on the floor and dropped a curtain that unveiled a Wheaties box that must have stood at least fifteen feet high. I think this was the first time I really accepted the reality of this honor. One of my favorite parts of the Wheaties reunion in El Paso was how happy my teammates were for me that I was on the cover. No one questioned why I was on the cover instead of them. I could tell all the congratulations were genuine and that meant so much to me. As teammates, they still all had my back. When I returned to New York, I went to the supermarket and took a trip down the cereal aisle. I wanted to actually see a box up on the shelves. When I did, I took it down and started shaking it. It was almost like I didn't really believe they actually put food in these things. Part of me kind of wanted a manager to hear that there was a crazy man shaking a box of cereal in aisle three, so that when he asked me what I was doing I could show him my picture and say, "This is me."

The movie *Glory Road* was the number one film in the country for several weeks. It was a box office success. But even after it left the theatres, the Wheaties box kept our story out there just a little bit longer. As I said earlier, 2006 was a whirlwind year.

Towards the end of the year, I got another call from Steve and, once again, I couldn't let myself believe that what he was telling me could be true. He was putting together an application for our Texas Western team's nomination for the Naismith Memorial Basketball Hall of Fame. Steve was really the driving force behind our application and you really have to understand that this was a big undertaking. I still have a copy of the application, and it looks like a paper that a student has to turn in to get their Ph.D. Steve put together biographies on all of the players and summarized various reasons why the team merited consideration.

Harry Flournoy, one of our team captains, checked in with me and I remember him saying, "Will, I think we have a real chance at this." He pointed out that if we were inducted, we'd be the first collegiate team to ever get this honor. A handful of teams had been inducted previously, but never a college one. That fact actually made me feel very skeptical about our chances for induction. If I had a vote, I'd put in U.C.L.A. They won a million championships. Shouldn't they get in before us? But Harry, and Steve, reminded me not to discount the historical significance of our win over Kentucky.

Weeks went by and I continued to keep the concept of getting into the Hall of Fame out of my mind. Then, Steve called. He gave me the news that the 1966 Texas Western Miners made it. We made it! We were going into the Hall of Fame as a team. I dug down deep to my Willie Worsley Bronx roots and tried to sound as cool as could be. I thanked Steve for all he had done, while sounding like this news was just another day at the office. But of course it wasn't. When I hung up the phone, I jumped around, screamed at the top of my lungs, and cried. I was so happy, Cloud Nine happy, and my tears were tears of joy. I know there is a reward waiting for me in heaven, but this was going to be my reward on earth. I was so happy for everyone: my teammates, the team trainers, the city of El Paso and, of course, Coach Don Haskins. Don Haskins had already been inducted as a coach, but I loved that he would be enshrined again with us. The man got death threats for starting five black players. He was a trailblazer. I looked over at my phone, ignored it, and sat down on my couch. I didn't call a soul. There was a part of me that thought there had to be a mistake. I thought I'd jinx myself. I figured once I told someone, Steve would call back and apologize for the big mistake that had been made.

The next morning I woke up for work and saw some big news on ESPN's Sportscenter. On the crawl at the bottom of the screen, they were displaying all the new Hall of Fame inductees, and I saw Texas Western with my own two eyes. It was there for me in living color, and I finally was able to accept that it was real. I called Roz and joked that we were going to take a trip up to her neck of the woods, since she went to college in New England.

On September 7th, 2007, Texas Western went to Springfield for the ultimate honor in sports—a Hall of Fame induction. We were one of seven inductees. W.N.B.A. Coach Van Chancellor, referee Mendy Rudolph, European coach Pedro Fernandez, N.B.A. coach Phil Jackson, International coach Mirko Novosel, and college coach Roy Williams also got the same call we did.

You cannot imagine what it felt like to be a V.I.P. in a room filled with a combination of the greatest players and coaches of all time. We were given seats on the floor, right down by the stage, on the good side of the ropes, and the list of people with worse seats than me would amaze you. Before the ceremony, I got to catch up with Kareem about our time as teenagers in the Bronx. I chatted with Walt "Clyde" Frazier, and even had a nice talk with fellow inductee Roy Williams. We talked about how different the work regimens of players these days were compared to how us old timers used to exercise. I was having a great time.

One of the great rewards of induction is receiving a Hall of Fame ring. When I got mine, in a beautiful box, I quickly put it my pocket. Roz was with me and demanded that I put it on. She wanted to see it on my finger. I gave in, but when she turned her back, I quickly returned it to the box and my pocket. I think it was the old-school Bronx in me. Where I grew up, you could never wear something like this on the subway and plan to have it very long. If a group approached you and wanted your ring, they would get the ring… and take your finger along with it if that's what it took. I eventually gave it to Roz, as I mentioned earlier in the book, for safe keeping. I'm glad it's hers. Another amazing souvenir was a blue blazer Hall of Fame jacket. When I put it on, it didn't fit. I think they must have used the height and weight from a 1966 Texas Western home game program. They still thought I was 'Wee" Willie Worsley. That's ok with me. It's not something I would wear around anyway, probably for the same reasons I didn't want to wear my ring. Whether it fits or not, the jacket is mine and something I will treasure forever.

Harry Flournoy was, and still is, one of my best friends in the world. When we were brought on stage for our honor, there was no doubt that he would be the one to give the speech. Harry has done a lot of public speaking engagements in his efforts to send a positive message to young people. I am so proud of the things he said that night. He did a wonderful job. I asked Harry if he would mind me including a copy of his speech in this book. Harry, who would do anything in the world for me, didn't take two seconds before saying yes. The reason I want to include the speech here is that if you've read this book up to this point, you can really appreciate his words. Harry said:

"First of all, I want to thank the Hall of Fame for this great honor….

In 1966, we had seven black players, four white players, and one Hispanic player. And our only purpose was to be the best team in the country. We did not have a social agenda at that time. We were only thinking about winning the championship. We thought we had the best team in the country. We knew that the following year, there was a team with a young man on it, I can't think of his name now—they said if freshmen could play that U.C.L.A. would have won it that year. But let me tell you something, we were determined. And I'm sorry Kareem, but we would have beat you guys that year too. (His joke got great laughs from the crowd)

We worked hard together on the court, and we had a lot of fun together off the court. All of us! We weren't separated. There wasn't three blacks or four blacks over here and the whites there and the Hispanic player there…we were together not only as a team – but we were like brothers. And like I said, we didn't have a social agenda. But God had a hand in that and he chose us to open doors. He chose us to open the door to all people. Not just African Americans, but to all people who were oppressed. All people who were having doors slammed in their face because of race, or gender, or any other reason. He chose us. And we handled that. We handled that as a team.

There are so many people that we have to thank for helping us get through that season -- Coach Haskins and Coach Iba. They were dedicated and they worked hard. They worked us to make us a team. You can't just put talented people out there and think you're going to win some games. It takes dedication. It takes discipline. It takes direction. And he gave that to us.

Jerry Bruckheimer, Jim Gartner, The Walt Disney family and the cast and crew of *Glory Road*. We thank them for putting out an outstanding movie. And not compromising us in the process. We give them a lot of thanks. Steven B. Tredennick. We always thought -- I wonder what the B. stood for? I know it stands for "Busy" now because he's the one who made this possible. He asked the question -- all these awards that we've been getting-- why not the Hall of Fame? Why not the Hall of Fame? And then he set out and worked hard and made this a reality.

We thank Joe Gomez -- a forgotten person in this. But Joe Gomez, twenty some odd years ago decided that we were not going to be forgotten for what we've done -- not only for the city of El Paso, but for the whole country. And he had a reunion that was so successful that we had to have several more after that. We want you to understand this. Understand that we did what we did because it was necessary. When you go back into those days and you know that these guys played hard -- and we played the game because it was an escape for us. It was an escape from the realities of the times. It was when people would tell you what you couldn't do. People would tell you that you can't put five black players out on the floor at the same time. Then you'd ask the question why -- because they're black. You can't have five black players out there and think that one of them is going to lead the team. Why -- because they're black. If you put five black players out there, when the game gets tight they're going to quit on you. Why -- because they're black. We had to break that. We proved that a farce -- a fallacy.

But we also know that it wasn't just about the black players on that team. It was about the whole team. Because sometimes the four white players and one Hispanic player are forgotten. But unless all of us worked together, we would not have accomplished what we did. We're so glad when we look at today's game and we see the diversity in today's game. It does our hearts good. But we want you to understand one thing: it's a commitment you have to make to give back to that game. It's not about the money. It's not about the material things. Those are highly overrated. It's about giving back the things that were given to you.

We thank you again for this great honor. We will always cherish this. We want you to understand this also -- all things are possible. You only have to believe. Thank you again."

Harry is an amazing man.

As exciting as the Hall of Fame night was for me, it was in some ways bittersweet. I made it to the Hall of Fame because of my friend, my brother, Bobby Joe Hill. But here I was at the Hall of Fame without my friend, my brother, Bobby Joe Hill. It didn't seem right. He should be here and I was sad that he wasn't. However, one thing happened that night that helped me deal with these feelings. I forgot to tell you the last line of Harry's speech. Before we left the stage, Harry looked out into the audience of basketball hall of famers, then gave a quick look to the sky and said:

"Bobby Joe—We're home! God Bless You!"

Chapter 18: Our Reward Will be in History

"What you are as a person is far more important than what you are as a basketball player."

-John Wooden

    I'm guessing that I met Lee Cutler towards the tail end of 2010, or maybe the very beginning of 2011. Lee is the vice-president of our union in Albany and he was in our area visiting some of the schools in Rockland. Maybe because of the movie *Glory Road*, or maybe because of The Hall of Fame induction, he made a special effort to stop by and introduce himself to me. He was a very nice man and we hit it off right away. I invited him to come to watch one of our basketball scrimmages and he took me up on the offer. We stayed in touch and he eventually had the idea that the N.E.A. newsletter, which stands for the National Education Association, should do an article on me. The two or three page piece focused in on many of the things I've written about in this book—my transition from an N.C.A.A. champion to my time working with young people. I was flattered and honored about the piece, but little did I know that one of the most amazing honors of my life would come from this.

    On July 11th, 2011, I flew to Chicago, Illinois for the 2011 Human and Civil Rights Awards. Lee Cutler nominated me, and the N.E.A. presented me with the H. Councill Trenholm Memorial Award for my lifetime in human services. I cannot describe how much this means to me. And I say to you, dear reader, with all sincerity, that this honor means even more to me than my Hall of Fame induction. As John Wooden said, "What you are as a person is far more important that what you are as a basketball player."

    I was not the only person being honored that night. Two state senators, Henry Marsh and Mary Jane Garcia were also honored, along with about ten others. Kerri Kennedy, daughter of Robert Kennedy, and niece of former president John F. Kennedy, was one of the recipients. Ms. Kennedy travels around the world trying to give a voice to people who are in need. She is involved in many amazing charities, and this was in recognition of her great philanthropic work. My mother, Julia, almost didn't let me go to Texas Western in El Paso because of the J.F.K assassination. Now here I was, in 2011, forty-seven years later, being honored on the same stage as J.F.K.'s niece. It felt good knowing how proud my mother would have been to see me receive this incredible award.

    The N.E.A. sent a film crew to follow me around for a few days in order to get some footage for a montage to be shown at the ceremony. I was very touched by all the nice things that were said about me.

My brother from another mother, Syd McGready, was the first person shown in the video. As my long-time friend and volunteer at Spring Valley, he was asked to say something about me. Syd said, "When Willie's team won the N.C.A.A., it was an earth-shattering, momentous occasion, because it was the first time five black players had started a game against five white players. It really brought a revolution and a realization to the sporting world about the need to recognize black athletes and to integrate the schools." How am I going to make it through this video? I am already getting emotional and the montage just started.

Next, they interviewed my friend, and Spring Valley Athletic Director, Bill Pilla.
Bill said, "He's a living legend here. We all know he was on the Texas Western team. He was on the cover of the Wheaties box. He's an unbelievable coach." When words like that come from someone you have so much respect for, it really means a lot.

Karen Pinel, the principal of Spring Valley High School said, "Not only is he an outstanding coach but an outstanding human being. He really creates a family for the boys that are on the team." Those are kind and supportive words from a kind and supportive person and a great principal. If I try really hard, I might be able to give my speech without crying.

Lee Cutler, the person who nominated me was the next to be shown in the video. I am so glad that he was asked to speak, because he was the driving force behind me receiving this honor. Lee said, "Willie is here to inspire these kids in this school district, who really start out with very little, and to get out the message that it doesn't matter if you come from poverty. It doesn't matter the color of your skin. You can succeed. And Willie is a testimony to that."

Andrew Delva is a teaching assistant at Spring Valley High School. He is also our Head Football Coach and Head Coach of our Boys Track and Field team. I have worked as a coach for the Girls' Track team, in addition to my varsity basketball position. Andrew and I work together with our athletes, but that is not our only connection. Andrew Delva is a former Spring Valley student and he played for me my first year as a basketball coach at the school. Andrew, also a football player, has the build of an offensive lineman. If there was such a thing as a gentle brick wall, it would be him. He is such a nice young man, but he certainly has an intimidating physical presence. He was my rebounder and enforcer on the team. One look at him made many teams second guess trying to drive through the lane. Kevin Bullock, the student who allowed Roz to help him with his foul shooting, also coaches football in our district and is friends with Coach Delva. I sometimes work the sideline markers at football games, and one time I noticed, before a big game between their teams, Andrew and Kevin at mid-field with big smiles on their faces chatting away. I walked out to them and told them how proud I was of both of them. I knew one of their teams would win that day, and the other would lose. But seeing two of my former players, whom I respect so much as men, come back to the district and do such great things with the students made me tell them that, "On this day, I am a winner no matter what happens." On the video, Andrew said, "It was a big thing for me seeing another man of color being successful. He's helping people of color to go to school, get an education, come back, and do something good with the community, which I've done."

Chanze Wellington is one of my former players. I don't know how they tracked him down, but I'm glad they did. Chanze is one of those rare people whom everyone likes. You can't find someone with a bad word to say about Chanze. On the video, he said about me, "He was able to convey to me that there are life lessons in basketball. There are things you can use in basketball that you can use in your daily life. Even to this day, the same principles that I learned in playing basketball I use right now, which is why I feel like I'm having some success in my life after basketball." Chanze was being modest about his success as a Spring Valley graduate. He is now a lawyer.

Richard Ianuzzi, the President of the New York State United Teachers Union, was also featured in the video. He said, "Willie Worsley is a legend. He's an example of what N.Y.S.E.D. (New York State Education Department) is about. He's an example of what N.E.A. is about. He's an example of real leadership and a real role model."

The video also showed footage of me in the halls of Spring Valley and on the basketball court and track field with students. They also showed me giving a talk to one of the classes at the school, and I was happy to see my good friend, and excellent teacher, Michele Bond, in the video. Michele has always been one of my biggest supporters at Spring Valley, so when I watched the video from my seat in the auditorium it was great to see her friendly face. She means a lot to me.

During these days of shooting footage around Spring Valley High School, I was asked a lot of "philosophy on life" type questions. Since I was receiving this award, they wanted to get insight into my approach to working in human services. One of the quotes they used has me saying, "What I teach them is what I learned from experience. If you don't have hope, you're in trouble. If you don't have hope, it's like running in quicksand. You'll go down quickly. You have to give them hope. You have to give them the idea that the glass is half full. Never give up." Of all the things I said over those days, I'm glad they used that quote. In human services, you need to make people believe that they can improve any situation.

The M.C. of the event went to the microphone after the video was complete and said, "Whether they call him a Hall of Famer, a coach, an activist, or a legend, we're proud to call him one of our own. Ladies and Gentlemen, the winner of the 2011 H. Councill Trenholm Memorial award -- Willie Worsley." I felt like I just won an Academy Award. I floated to the stage, made sure to thank my union, co-workers, and all the students and players who let me be a part of their lives. And, of course, I thanked the N.E.A. for this meaningful award that will always be close to my heart. I closed my comments by mentioning that I felt grateful and humble to be among all the outstanding people that were there that evening. When I was finished, I floated back to my seat and enjoyed the rest of the night, amazed by life.

In 1997, I sat in my office at the Harlem Boys and Girls Choir school with author Frank Fitzpatrick. Frank was working on a book that he would eventually publish in 1999 called *And the Walls Came Tumbling Down*. The book chronicles the events leading up to, and the aftermath of, the 1966 N.C.A.A. Championship game between Texas Western and Kentucky. Frank reached out to former players and he and I had spoken on several occasions. Frank was a great guy, very genuine and straightforward, and he thanked me and included me on his acknowledgements page when the book was published. I really appreciated that and I think that most people interested in the topic of our famous game look at Frank's book as the premiere work on the subject.

On that day, Frank asked me something to the effect of whether or not I felt Texas Western had gotten enough recognition for our historic win. I think the premise for the question was based on a lot of factors, including the false rumors spread about the education of the Texas Western players, to the racial taunts we endured during the season, to the death threats received by Coach Haskins. Those are things not every team has to go through. I looked across my desk and said, "People say your reward will be in Heaven, but our reward will be in history." I didn't realize at the time just how true that quote would turn out to be. Nine years after I said it, the movie *Glory Road* was released. Ten years after I said it, Texas Western was inducted into the Hall of Fame. Fourteen years after I said it, I was honored at the 2011 Human and Civil Rights Awards ceremony. "Our reward will be in history" was a quote that stuck and I saw in print again when the movie and Hall of Fame honors were happening. It was also shown during the video awards montage made for me in 2011. And even though I said that quote about the famous basketball game in 1966, I think it applies just as much, for me, to the 2011 H. Councill Trenholm Memorial award. If a person ever looks back at the history of Willie Worsley, they will see not only the basketball honors and tributes, but also the recognition of my desire to fulfill my lifelong dream of helping others.

There are many different reasons someone might sit down and write a book about their life. I had one reason for writing this book -- my grandchildren. Believe it or not, when they read this book they will actually learn a lot of things about me that they might not have known already. And I would want them, or any other young person reading this book, to be educated about what I have learned through all the amazing experiences I've had. Do your best in life. Always stay hopeful and true. Make a positive difference in the lives of others and never stop. The reward for these efforts might not come tomorrow. The reward for these things might not be seen next week. But it will come. I want them to know that it will come. Sometimes, our reward will be in history!

Chapter 19: The Greatest Game of My Life

"Grandpa, you are my inspiration because you are good at what you do. You are a caring and loving person who loves to help people. You are not selfish and you are good at teaching people things."

- Kayla Worsley Wooten

"Papa, I hope you know how much I admire you. You have been through so much and always come out strong. No matter what is going on in life, you can still put a smile on people's faces

- Mahogany Worsley Wooten

Earlier in the book, I mentioned an annual fundraiser tournament called The Willie Worsley Shootout. The fundraiser helps the Spring Valley Varsity players to get sweat suits to be worn on game days. It's also a fun reason to get people together and play basketball, and by this point in the book, you have probably figured out that I am a big fan of that.

For years, the tournament only featured boys teams. But a couple of years ago, we thought it might be a good idea to get some girls involved in the fun. It was a nice event and six of the eleven schools in the county had at least one player representing them.

This year was going to be the most special Willie Worsley Shootout of them all for me. I was going to coach one of the girls' teams, and my granddaughters, Brianana and Mahogany, were going to be on the squad with their sister, Kayla, in the stands cheering them on.

Matt Greenbaum is the coach of the East Ramapo girls' team and another good friend of mine. He is someone I also consider one of my biggest supporters at Spring Valley High School. As the tournament went on, his team was scheduled to face the team of players assembled for me to coach. It was a funny feeling for me to walk into the Spring Valley gym and see him and his players on the home bench. This never happened to me before. I was on the visiting bench on my home court, and I got a big kick out of that. Somehow, the game ended up going into overtime. Mahogany was only in sixth or seventh grade at the time, so all the other girls were bigger and quicker than she was. Then out of nowhere, Mahogany pressed up on one of the girls. She stole the ball and made a lay-up. The buzzer sounded and we won the game. I could tell by her reaction that she didn't even realize what happened. She was still just so excited to be playing with the big kids. The girls, including Brianana who was on the court at the time too, swarmed Mahogany and the celebrating began. Even Kayla, who is obligated by the laws of being a twin to give Mahogany the business when she can, ran onto the court and hugged and kissed her. Those were the only points Mahogany scored the whole game. And, as usual, I tried to play it cool, but my heart nearly jumped out of my chest. It was a true Kodak moment.

The next day at school, part of me wanted to steer clear of Matt. Like me, he has the competitive nature you need as a coach. If someone is keeping score, he and I both want to win. And it is this drive that will make Matt a successful coach long after I've retired. But Matt is a gentleman. He gave me genuine congratulations on the win. I think he knew how much it meant to me to have a chance to coach my girls.

I have been interviewed by journalists for close to fifty years now. Many times, I've been asked about the greatest game of my life -- referring to the 1966 Texas Western Championship. But the greatest basketball moment of my life happened when Mahogany sank that shot in the Willie Worsley Shootout. When you become a parent, and then a grandparent, your individual accomplishments all become secondary. There is nothing more important than your family. The greatest game of my life is the game of life. My biggest victory is seeing Etta's children: David, Nicole, and Michael thrive in this world. My biggest victory is seeing Roz's children: Brianana, Mahogany, and Kayla thrive in this world. Maybe someday one of my grandkids will play high school or college basketball, maybe even in an N.C.A.A. championship just like I did, and I will be in the stands as a fan. I won't be there as Willie Worsley the N.C.A.A. Champion, Basketball Hall of Famer, or coach. I will be there as Willie Worsley, grandpa. And that dream warms my heart. I have played in, and coached, thousands of basketball games, -- but I know in my heart that the greatest game of my life hasn't even been played yet.

Acknowledgements

To my family and Terry, there are so many things I could say in the form of thanks. My hope is that you "live as long as you want and never want as long as you live." Thank You – Thank You!
With Love Always,
Coach!!

I have many people to thank for their help with my work on this book. Of course, I need to start with Mr. Worsley. Thank you for allowing me to be a part of this project. This is a highlight of my life and I treasure every amazing story you told me during our times together after school.

I'd like to thank Mr. Worsley's family for putting their trust in me to work on his memoir. This book would not have happened without their vote of confidence. In addition, I'd like to thank Mr. Worsley's close friends Nate "Tiny" Archibald, Harry Flournoy, and Syd McGready for their help.

I'd like to thank my beautiful wife Jen for always supporting me, and also for being a great editor. I had additional help from several of my dear friends: Mike Reiter also edited and helped revise this book. I owe him a great deal of thanks for his work. Dave Warren gave me invaluable advice, observations, and support. I'd like to thank Malachy Donoghue for instilling in me an appreciation for a great autobiography. Thank you Kelli Novotny for the beautiful book cover and dedication page. Thank you Andy Chalfin and Marielle Reiter Poss for your advice. My friend Mike "Jakes" Jacobs loves basketball more than anyone on the planet. If you woke Jakes up at three in the morning he could tell you every stat of the 1983 New Jersey Nets. His enthusiasm about this book was always appreciated.

I'd like to thank all my friends at Spring Valley High School. In particular, thank you Michele Bond, Chris Ferraro, and Morose Leonard for your suggestions.

Finally, I have to thank my amazing daughters Erin and Marissa for the happiness they bring me every day. I hope when they read this book, they learn the same lessons from Mr. Worsley that I did: Handle every challenge with class and dignity, always work to help others, and believe that with hope, hard work, and perseverance, anything is possible.

Terry Mulgrew

Made in the USA
Lexington, KY
13 April 2015